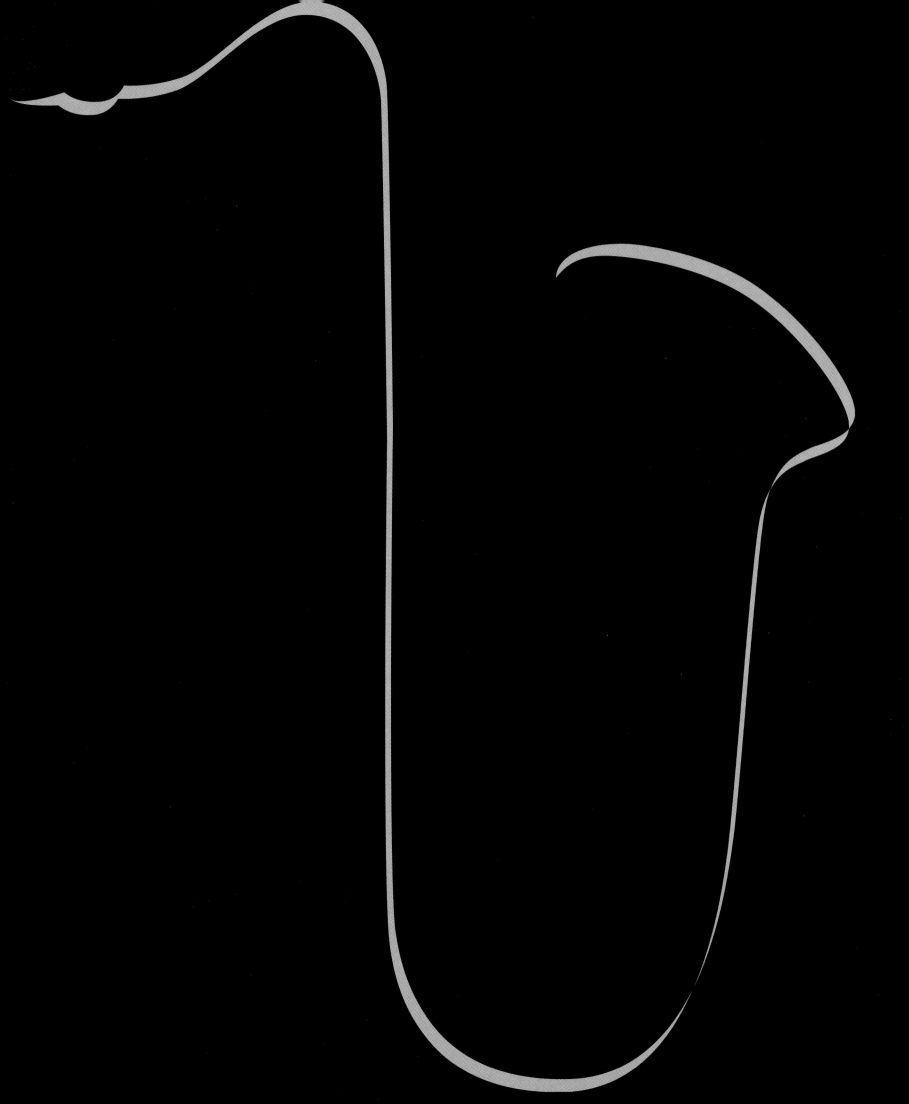

TEXT
BILL MILKOWSKI

FOREWORD
JOE LOVANO

PROJECT EDITOR
VALERIA MANFERTO DE FABIANIS

EDITORIAL COORDINATION
LAURA ACCOMAZZO - GIORGIA RAINERI

GRAPHIC DESIGN
MARINELLA DEBERNARDI

CONTENTS

FOREWORD BY JOE LOVANO PAGE 8

INTRODUCTION PAGE 10

JELLY ROLL MORTON The Inventor of Jazz? PAGE 18

LOUIS ARMSTRONG Jazz's First Solo Genius PAGE 22

SIDNEY BECHET Star Soloist of Soprano Sax PAGE 32

BIX BEIDERBECKE Jazz Age Trumpet Phenom PAGE 38

DUKE ELLINGTON Elegant Maestro, Jazz Ambassador PAGE 42

CAB CALLOWAY His Hi-De-Highness of Ho-De-Ho PAGE 52

FATS WALLER Ebullient Jivester, Stride Stylist PAGE 60

DJANGO REINHARDT Europe's First Jazz Star PAGE 64

COUNT BASIE Swinging the Blues PAGE 66

CHICK WEBB Sultan of the Savoy Ballroom PAGE 70

BENNY GOODMAN The King of Swing PAGE 72

CHARLIE CHRISTIAN Electric Guitar Pioneer PAGE 80

LIONEL HAMPTON Jammer, Jivester, Pioneering Vibist PAGE 82

GENE KRUPA Flamboyant Drummin' Man PAGE 88

BILLIE HOLIDAY Lady Sings the Blues PAGE 92

COLEMAN HAWKINS The Song of the Hawk PAGE 98

LESTER YOUNG President of the Tenor Saxophone PAGE 100

CHARLIE PARKER High-Flying Bird and the Birth of Bebop PAGE 104

DIZZY GILLESPIE Bebop Architect, Latin Jazz Innovator PAGE 106

THELONIOUS MONK The High Priest of Bebop PAGE 114

ART TATUM Virtuoso of the Highest Order PAGE 118

SARAH VAUGHAN The Divine One   PAGE 120

ELLA FITZGERALD First Lady of Song   PAGE 128

BUDDY RICH 'The World's Greatest Drummer'   PAGE 136

MAX ROACH Bebop Pioneer, Musical Drummer   PAGE 138

MILES DAVIS The Picasso of Jazz   PAGE 144

BUD POWELL The Charlie Parker of Piano   PAGE 156

BILL EVANS New Impressions for Piano   PAGE 158

SONNY ROLLINS Saxophone Colossus   PAGE 164

JOHN COLTRANE Giant Steps to the New Thing   PAGE 172

ART BLAKEY The Indestructible Bu   PAGE 176

HORACE SILVER Father of Funky Hard Bop   PAGE 180

STAN GETZ The Sound, the Swing, the Samba   PAGE 184

DAVE BRUBECK Adventures in Time   PAGE 190

CHET BAKER Poignant Tones, Ravaged Life   PAGE 194

CHARLES MINGUS Formidable Bassist, Prolific Composer   PAGE 202

ORNETTE COLEMAN Sax Revolutionary, Free Jazz Icon   PAGE 208

JIMMY SMITH The Original Hammond B-3 Burner   PAGE 214

WES MONTGOMERY Heir to Charlie Christian's Throne   PAGE 218

FREDDIE HUBBARD Baddest Trumpet Man on the Planet   PAGE 220

HERBIE HANCOCK Crossing the Electro-Acoustic Divide   PAGE 222

WAYNE SHORTER The Enigmatic Mr. Gone   PAGE 226

JOE ZAWINUL Visionary Keyboardist, Fusion Innovator   PAGE 232

CHICK COREA No Mystery to his Mastery   PAGE 234

JOHN MCLAUGHLIN A Bona Fide Guitar Avatar   PAGE 240

JACO PASTORIUS 'The World's Greatest Bass Player?   PAGE 244

PAT METHENY New Horizons for Jazz Guitar   PAGE 248

KEITH JARRETT The Art of the Improviser   PAGE 254

WYNTON MARSALIS 21st Century Jazz Ambassador   PAGE 258

JOE LOVANO In the Tradition, to the Future   PAGE 264

INDEX   PAGE 268

FOREWORD

BY JOE LOVANO

Throughout history the myths and legends of mankind have inspired us, shaped what is to be and given us a picture of what was. The present moment is the dimension we live in but to develop as artists we must embrace the masters of our craft and learn from their experiences and passions. Among the legendary musical personalities throughout history, it is arguable that the Jazz style has produced the most colorful and inspired musicians, singers, composers and entertainers that they have emerged during the last century of recorded music.

"Legends of Jazz" represents a microcosm of the characters and personalities that have shaped this joyous music and amazing art form. Their sounds, ideas and spirits loom large and are timeless!! Jazz is full of love, passion, imagination, intellect, compassion, spirituality, humor, realism, vision, self awareness and the social environment that surrounds and fuels all of the stories that are expressed in the music.

In Jazz and improvised music there are many stories that relate to everyday life. Everyone's feelings, sounds and personal approach are what make the music come alive. Each contribution inspires others to develop, which is so important to the continuum of the music, so that future generations can emerge on their own terms.

What makes a legend throughout history has been a wild passion that is indefinable. This is a spiritual music that is honest and comes from your soul... All of the Legends and Jazz Masters listed here, from Jelly Roll Morton onwards, have that in common.

4 | Louis Armstrong, the first genius improviser in jazz who single-handedly revolutionized music with his Hot Five and Hot Seven sessions from 1925-1927, pictured in 1970. 9 | Tenor saxophonist-composer-bandleader Joe Lovano, a perennial poll-winner and the face of jazz for a generation, performing at the 2010 North Sea Jazz Festival.

INTRODUCTION

Born in America, the product of a confluence of circumstance and influence, jazz emerged at the dawn of the 20th century and has continued to evolve ever since. And like other great rivers, numerous tributary streams continue to feed the main channel along the way.

The eminent critic Whitney Balliet once called it "the sound of surprise" while the music's first superstar, Louis Armstrong, cryptically opined, when queried about the definition of jazz: "Man, if you gotta ask, you'll never know."

According to another of its most prominent stars, Miles Davis, "Jazz has got to have that *thing*. You have to be born with it. You can't learn it, you can't buy it. You have it or you don't. And no critic can put it into any words. It speaks in the music. It speaks for itself."

New Orleans soprano sax virtuoso Sidney Bechet once noted about jazz, "You know, there's this mood about the music, a kind of need to be moving. You just can't set it down and hold it. Those Dixieland musicianers, they tried to do that; they tried to write the music down and kind of freeze it. Even when they didn't arrange it to death, they didn't have any place to send it; that's why they lost it. You just can't keep the music unless you move with it."

Or more to the point, as Art Blakey famously said, "Jazz washes away the dust of everyday life."

Balliet's epithet for jazz — the sound of surprise — applies as readily to Armstrong's landmark duets with Earl Hines in 1928 as it does to Charlie Parker's blistering bebop flights on 52nd Street with Dizzy Gillespie in 1945, Davis' modal excursions with John Coltrane in 1959, Joe Zawinul's pan-global experiments with Weather Report in the 1970s and 1980s, John Zorn's provocative merging of Jewish klezmer music with Ornette Coleman-inspired music during the 1990s or Joe Lovano's radical reinvention of Charlie Parker themes with his US Five group in 2011.

So where did this mysterious, magical improvisational art form come from? It could've happened in no other place than New Orleans. By the early 1800s, the Crescent City was one of the richest, most cosmopolitan and integrated cities in America. It was in this nexus of melodies from the West Indies, polyrhythms and call-and-response traditions brought over by slaves from West Africa, and the European classical influence brought into the cultural gumbo through the various opera companies and sophisticated, classically-trained Creole musicians that jazz was born. Add a thriving brass band tradition, which developed in the late 19th century from the plentiful supply of cheap brass band instruments left behind after the Civil War, the infectious habanera rhythms imported from Cuba and the Caribbean (the so-called "Spanish tinge" that Jelly Roll Morton said inhabited his music) and the raucous party-time atmosphere of "laissez les bons temps bouler ("Let the good times roll") that has always permeated New Orleans and you have a potent recipe for the creation of a new, exciting hybrid musical form.

Ragtime was a forerunner of jazz. Derived from brass band music and European folk melodies along with African-American banjo music and spirituals, minstrel songs, military marches and European light classics, it was a syncopated, toe-tapping piano music that was strictly through-composed and involved only limited improvisation. The emergence of ragtime coincided with the invention of cheap, mass-produced pianos, which had become all the rage for an upwardly mobile middle class. And, of course, all of those pianos required sheet music. Enter John Stark, an entrepreneur in a small music-publishing firm, who struck a deal with Scott Joplin over the rights to his music. Joplin's sheet music sold in unprecedented numbers during the ragtime era. His most popular work, "Maple Leaf Rag," sold 75,000 copies in 1899 and gradually became a nationwide sensation, selling upwards of a million copies within a few years, becoming a 'must have' for other aspiring pianists.

Joplin's classically-inspired yet brightly syncopated piano playing directly informed the work of early jazz piano pioneers like Jelly Roll Morton, James P. Johnson, Willie "The Lion" Smith and Fats Waller. Joplin saw himself as a black American counterpart to Chopin or Strauss composing syncopated sonatas for the masses. He reigned as the "King of Ragtime Writers" for nearly 20 years until his death in 1917, the same year that the first recording by the Original Dixieland Jass Band was made (initially, the term was spelled 'jass' and only later came to be spelled 'jazz').

By 1917, the exploits of cornetist Charles "Buddy" Bolden were legendary. A powerful, pioneering player in jazz history, Bolden was leading his own group as early as 1895. People from that period spoke of being able to hear Bolden's strong trumpet tones blocks away from the picnics that he played in Lincoln Park at the turn of the century. His popularity spread throughout New Orleans from playing dance halls and venues like Preservation Hall, the Tin Roof Café and Funky Butt Hall, but by 1903 he was already off the scene. Plagued by alcoholism and incapacitated by schizophrenia, he was committed, in 1907, to the Louisiana State Insane Asylum, where he spent the rest of his life before passing away on November 4, 1931.

Bolden's 'trumpet king' banner was picked up by Freddie Keppard, who led the Olympia Orchestra in 1906. Another of the city's early trumpet kings, Joe Oliver, joined the Onward Brass Band in 1904 and by 1917 had become the star cornetist in Kid Ory's band.

An early master of mutes, Oliver pioneered the "wah-wah" and other vocal effects on his horn. By the time he left New Orleans in February, 1919, and headed north to Chicago, he was billed as Joe "King" Oliver. Three years later, he was joined in the Windy City by his young protégé Louis Armstrong, who had come north to join Oliver in his Creole Jazz Band and changed the course of jazz history in the process.

As New Orleans had been the birthplace of jazz at the turn of the century, so Chicago became the hotbed of jazz in the 1920s, which the influential American author F. Scott Fitzgerald dubbed "The Jazz Age." Louis Armstrong's historic Hot Five and Hot Seven sessions recorded between 1925 and 1928 fueled the new movement of 'hot jazz.' By 1929, Armstrong had shifted his home base from Chicago to New York, where jazz was poised for its next evolution.

Following the Depression (1929-1933), jazz hit a peak of popularity during the so-called Swing era, which had reached fever pitch by 21 August 1935 when Benny Goodman's triumph, at the Palomar Ballroom before a packed house of ecstatic teenagers, signaled the beginning of a new national youth craze. Goodman and other big bands led by Count Basie, Chick Webb, who reigned at the Savoy Ballroom in Harlem, Duke Ellington, whose residency at the Cotton Club helped make him a star, Cab Calloway, who followed Ellington's tenure at the Cotton Club, and all the great white bandleaders of the era, including Artie Shaw, Glenn Miller, Woody Herman and the Dorsey Brothers (Tommy and Jimmy) kept America swinging through the 1930s and into the 1940s. As jazz critic Scott Yanow wrote: "There was a time from 1935-1946 when teenagers and young adults danced to jazz-oriented bands, when jazz orchestras dominated pop charts and when influential clarinetists were household names. This was the Swing era."

With each passing decade came a new innovation. The post-World War II years ushered in the birth of jump blues (spearheaded by Louis Jordan, T-Bone Walker and Roy Milton) and also bebop (pioneered by Charlie Parker, Dizzy Gillespie, Kenny Clarke and Max Roach). Naturally, there was some resentment from members of the earlier musical camps, who felt that their place was being usurped by the new Young Lions on the scene. Many of the Swing era elders felt particularly threatened by the bebop interlopers, causing some tension between the generations. Cab Calloway reputedly warned trumpeter Dizzy Gillespie about playing "that Chinese music" in his band. Similarly, Louis Armstrong had a hard time adjusting to the streamlined modern bebop, until finally publically embracing Gillespie in the late 1940s. Just as each new visual art movement tends to trump the previous one, so it has been throughout the history of jazz.

In 1949, Miles Davis' *Birth of the Cool* ushered in a more mellow, more relaxed movement in jazz, which was a direct reaction to the burning, up-tempo turbulence of the bebop movement which had preceded it. Such important new artists as pianists Dave Brubeck, Lennie Tristano and John Lewis, saxophonists Gerry Mulligan, Lee Konitz and Paul Desmond, trumpeters Chet Baker and Shorty Rogers came along to cool down the incendiary tempos of bebop with lush harmonies and mellow-toned improvisations. As British jazz critic John Fordham wrote: "It was an ethereal drifting cloud music that used French horns as well as regular jazz instruments, highly wrought arrangements and rich tone colors through which the soloists played in a measured, walking-on-eggshells manner."

In the early 1950s, the hard-driving, blues and gospel-inflected hard bop movement emerged as a reaction to the cool school, forged by such gritty, aggressively-swinging players as Art Blakey, Horace Silver, Wes Montgomery, Cannonball Adderley and Clifford Brown. Some landmark recordings during that period include Art Blakey's *Moanin'*, Horace Silver's *Finger Poppin'* and *Blowin' the Blues Away*, the Clifford Brown-Max Roach Quartet's *At Basin Street,* Hank Mobley's *Soul Station*, Booker Ervin's *Cookin',* Adderley's *Somethin' Else*, Sonny Rollins' *Saxophone Colossus*, Wes Montgomery's *The Incredible Jazz Guitar of Wes Montgomery* and *Smokin' at the Half Note*, Jimmy Smith's *The Sermon*, Lee Morgan's *Sidewinder* and the Art Farmer-Benny Golson Jazztet's *Meet the Jazztet*.

By the late 1950s, Miles Davis had kicked off a new tributary with his modal explorations on 1958's *Milestones* and 1959's *Kind of Blue* (the best-selling jazz album of all time). This method of playing modes or scales rather than chord progressions led to similarly expansive experiments by pianists Andrew Hill (1963's *Black Fire*) and Herbie Hancock (1964's *Empyrean Isles* and 1965's *Maiden Voyage*), tenor saxophonist John Coltrane (1964's *Crescent*) and pianist McCoy Tyner (1962's *Inception*).

Jazz revolutionaries like alto saxophonist Ornette Coleman and pianist Cecil Taylor pioneered a new musical movement in the late 1950s and early 1960s. Called "free jazz" or "the new thing," this provocative new music ignored keys, chord structures and time signatures while focusing on freely evolving melodies and a unique chemistry between band members that bordered on telepathy. Coleman led the way with his 1958 debut recording *Something Else!!!!* which he followed with two recordings in 1959 — *Tomorrow is the Question* and *The Shape of Jazz to Come*, the latter being called by critic Steve Huey "a watershed event in the genesis of avant-garde jazz, profoundly steering its future course and throwing down a gauntlet that some still haven't come to grips with." Each of those groundbreaking recordings involved the application of Coleman's harmolodics theory, in which harmony, melody, speed, rhythm, time and phrasing all have equal importance. Cecil Taylor himself explored new territory on 1956's forward-thinking *Jazz Advance* and 1958's volatile *Looking Ahead*. Their individual experiments in the avant-garde spurred on similar investigations into the 'new thing' by the free association forms of tenor saxophonists Archie Shepp, Pharoah Sanders and Albert Ayler, alto saxophonist Eric Dolphy and soprano saxophonist Steve Lacy. Their adventurous free jazz experiments were carried on in an audacious group of Chicago-based improvisers collectively known as the Association for the Advancement of Creative Musicians (AACM, formed in 1965) and whose early members included pianist Muhal Richard Abrams, drummer Steve McCall, saxophonists Anthony Braxton, Joseph Jarman and Henry Threadgill, violinist Leroy Jenkins, bassist Malachi Favors Maghostut, drummer Famoudou Don Moye and trombonist George Lewis.

By the mid 1960s, bands around New York like guitarist Larry Coryell's Free Spirits and flutist Jeremy Steig & The Satyrs began organically blending rock and jazz. These were jazz-educated musicians with dreams of extending the bebop or hard bop traditions (in Coryell's case, he came to New York in 1965 with the idea of becoming the next Wes Montgomery). But the confluence of musical ideologies at the time — John Coltrane's heightened jazz meeting the Beatles peace-and-love psychedelia — caused Coryell and many other musicians on the Greenwich Village scene of the mid 1960s to create a vibrant new hybrid music. Miles Davis began picking up the lead of rockers Jimi Hendrix and Sly Stone by the late 1960s and putting his own authoritative trumpet stylings on top of that bombastic foundation. With 1968's *Filles de Kilimanjaro*, Miles put a big toe in the fusion pool and he waded in a little farther on 1969's *In A Silent Way*, which included the new British guitar sensation John McLaughlin along with electric keyboardists Joe Zawinul and Chick Corea. And with 1970's tumultuous *Bitches Brew*, Miles dove headlong into the deep waters of fusion, opening the floodgates for the blending of jazz and rock for a generation of musicians who followed in his wake. Acclaimed Davis alumni such as Tony Williams, Joe Zawinul, John McLaughlin, and Chick Corea would go on to form their own respective fusion bands (Tony Williams Lifetime, formed in 1969, Joe Zawinul's Weather Report and McLaughlin's Mahavishnu Orchestra both formed in 1971, and Chick Corea's Return To Forever, formed in 1972), ushering in a golden era of fusion that lasted roughly through the mid 1970s.

The 1980s saw the rise of such inspired renegades as tenor saxophonist David Murray, guitarist James "Blood" Ulmer, alto saxophonist Arthur Blythe, Steve Coleman's funk-and-hip-hop influenced M-Base, alto saxophonists John Zorn and Tim Berne, guitarists Pat Metheny, Bill Frisell and John Scofield, and bassist Jaco Pastorius, each of whom took personal approaches to the music that drew on the jazz tradition while pushing the envelope in extreme ways. At the same time, trumpeter Wynton Marsalis led a movement of Young Lions that tried to return jazz to its traditional roots, based on a reverence for Louis Armstrong, Duke Ellington, Thelonious Monk and the fundamental, age-old art of swing.

The 1990s saw even more permutations of jazz with the emergence of neo-groovemeisters Medeski, Martin & Wood, who pioneered the so-called jam band scene with their mesmerizing brand of avant-funk, and by the innovations of such talented player-composers as trumpeter Dave Douglas, clarinetist Don Byron, tenor saxophonist David S. Ware, and guitarist Sonny Sharrock. European jazz artists, who have been contributing to the music since the time of Django Reinhardt and the Hot Club of Jazz during the mid 1930s, emerged as a potent force in the music during the 1990s on the strength of recordings by such artists as Polish trumpeter Tomasz Stanko, British baritone saxophonist John Surman, German trombonist Albert Mangelsdorff, British trumpeter Kenny Wheeler and a whole host of Italian jazz musicians including Enrico Rava, Robert Gatto, Maria Pia De Vito, Gianluigi Trovesi, Paolo Fresu and the Instabile Orchestra.

A myriad ethnic music influences have also filtered into the jazz stream over the past 30 years, brought by gifted musicians including Canadian soprano saxophonist Jane Bunnett, who played and recorded in Cuba, Panamanian pianist Danilo Perez, German pianist Alex von Schlippenbach, Denmark's Pierre Dorge's New Jungle Orchestra, Holland's Willem Breuker's Kollektief, Argentine pianist-composer-arranger Guillermo Klein, Czech bassist George Mraz, Cameroonian bassist Richard Bona, Cuban trumpeter Arturo Sandoval, Norwegian alto saxophonist Jan Gabarek, Armenian percussionist Arto Tuncboyacian, Dutch pianist Misha Mengelberg, Lithuanian pianist Vyacheslave Fanelin, Cuban piano sensation Gonzalo Rubalcaba, Tunisian oud player Anouar Brahem, Chinese pianist-composer Jon Jang, Indian alto saxophonist Rudresh Mahanthappa, Pakistani guitarist Fareed Haque, Chinese baritone saxophonist Fred Ho, Vietnamese guitarist Nguyen Le, Swedish keyboard player Esbjorn Svensson, Cuban saxophonist-clarinetist Paquito D'Rivera, Swiss-Dutch vocalist Susanne Abbuehl, Swiss pianist Irene Schweizer, Japanese pianist-composer and big bandleader Toshiko Akiyoshi, Indian percussionist Zakir Hussain, Japanese pianist Satoko Fujii, Norwegian keyboard player Bugge Wesselhoft, Puerto Rican saxophonist David Sanchez, Brazilian percussionist Airto Moreira, Australian bassist Nicki Parrott, Irish guitarist David O'Rourke and Indian percussionist Trilok Gurtu … the list goes on and on.

Over the course of 100-plus years, jazz has moved from the brothels of Storyville (New Orleans' red-light district between 1897 and 1917 and where Jelly Roll Morton had begun embellishing ragtime and light classics as early as 1902) and steamboats on the Mississippi River to the night clubs and dance halls of Chicago and New York and onwards to concert halls all over the world. From its beginnings in America, its migration to Europe and on to Asia, Africa, the Middle East, Latin America and all points on the planet, jazz keeps expanding, picking up new converts with each new inroad and absorbing new elements from each culture it permeates. The sound of jazz prevails and, like water, takes on the shape of each and every vessel it fills.

Perhaps drummer Jo Jones, part of Count Basie's All-American rhythm section of the 1930s and 1940s, put it best when he said, "What is jazz? The closest I can get to answering that is to say that jazz is playing what you feel. All jazz musicians express themselves through their instruments and they express the types of persons they are, the experiences they've had during the day, during the night before, during their lives. There is no way they can subterfuge their feelings."

In its infancy, around the beginning of the 20th century, jazz was dismissed by one pointed newspaper editorial as "a manifestation of a low streak in man's taste that has not yet come out in civilization's wash." Its demise and comeback has been reported in mainstream magazines more than a few times. A recent article in the *Wall Street Journal* ("Can Jazz Be Saved?") posited that the audience for America's great art form is withering away. Some have argued that New York is no longer the center of the jazz universe and that the new center is in Europe or India or somewhere else. Regardless of worldwide sales figures, the vital signs of jazz look good, the sound of surprise prevails … everywhere.

"Jazz isn't just me. It isn't just any one person who plays it. There'll always be Jazz. It doesn't stop with me, it doesn't stop anywhere. As long as there's melody and rhythm, there's jazz."

Sidney Bechet

JELLY ROLL MORTON

THE INVENTOR OF JAZZ?

By all accounts a braggart of epic proportions, New Orleans native Ferdinand Joseph Lamothe was the self-proclaimed inventor of jazz. A light-skinned Creole of African and French descent, he was born on 20 October 1890 and lived a nomadic life as a pimp, pool hustler, card shark, nightclub manager, fight promoter and itinerant musician. A prolific composer and solo pianist of dazzling virtuosity, Morton was also a gifted arranger whose adventurous writing was far ahead of its time.

As a boy, Morton studied classical piano and by age 14 he had begun playing at one of the "sporting houses" of the Storyville red-light district. He adopted the name "Jelly Roll Morton" and in 1905 began touring the Gulf Coast's black vaudeville circuit, blending elements of ragtime and classical music with minstrel songs, Argentine tangos and church hymns along with the brass band funeral marches and habanera rhythms from the Caribbean that he had heard on the streets of New Orleans as a child.

By 1908, the wandering minstrel ended up in Memphis, where he met composer and blues pioneer W.C. Handy. In 1911, Morton traveled to New York, where he met future Harlem stride piano greats James P. Johnson and Willie "The Lion" Smith. In 1914, he settled in Chicago and he began writing down his compositions for the first time in his career. His "Jelly Roll Blues," published in 1915, was arguably the first jazz composition to be put on sheet music. Morton relocated to California during the summer of 1917 and for the next five years worked his syncopated magic up and down the West Cost from Tijuana to Vancouver.

By 1923, at the height of the Hot Jazz craze, Morton was back in Chicago, where he watched the ascendancy of Joe "King" Oliver's Creole Jazz Band and its star cornetist, Louis Armstrong. Morton's five years in Chicago turned out to be an incredibly fertile period for him, resulting in such classic recordings as "Mr. Jelly Lord," "Sobbin' Blues" and "Milenburg Joys" (with a group of young white musicians known as the New Orleans Rhythm Kings). He also recorded solo piano pieces like "Wolverine Blues" and "The Joys" as well as duets with King Oliver on "Tom Cat Blues" and "King Porter Stomp." The peak of Morton's productive phase in Chicago came in 1926–1927 with his Red Hot Peppers, which featured such respected New Orleans musicians as trombonist Kid Ory, clarinetist Omer Simeon, banjoist Johnny St. Cyr and drummer Baby Dodds. Among their most famous recordings were "The Pearls," "Doctor Jazz," "Deadman Blues" and "Black Bottom Stomp."

19 | New Orleans legend Jelly Roll Morton, piano virtuoso, prolific composer and self-proclaimed inventor of jazz, in Chicago, circa 1923.

By 1928, the center of jazz had shifted to New York and Morton followed. He assembled a new edition of his Red Hot Peppers for some recordings on the Victor label. But by the early 1930s, with the advent of the big band era, Morton's style was considered old-fashioned. Unable to find work in New York, he moved to Washington D.C. in 1935 and tended bar at a small club in the black district. In 1938, folklorist Alan Lomax documented Morton in a series of remarkably revealing interviews detailing his colorful upbringing in New Orleans and his observations on the early days of jazz. (These recordings were released posthumously, most recently, in 2005, as an eight-CD boxed set entitled *The Complete Library of Congress Recordings*). He attempted a comeback in 1939, recording an all-star session for the

> "I have been robbed of three million dollars all told. Everyone today is playing my stuff and I don't even get credit. Kansas City style, Chicago style, New Orleans style hell, they're all Jelly Roll style."
>
> Jelly Roll Morton

Bluebird label with fellow New Orleans musicians Sidney Bechet, Sidney de Paris, Zutty Singleton, Henry "Red" Allen and Albert Nicholas, and recorded his last session in January 1940. Morton died at age 50 in Los Angeles on 10 July 1941. The life and times of this audacious figure in jazz were chronicled in the 1992 Broadway musical *Jelly's Last Jam*.

20-21 | Jelly Roll Morton and his Red Hot Peppers in Chicago, 1926 or 1927 (from left to right: trombonist Kid Ory, drummer Andrew Hilaire, trumpeter George Mitchell, bassist John Lindsay, Morton on piano, banjoist Johnny St. Cyr, clarinetist Omer Simeon).

21 | Jelly Roll Morton and his Red Hot Peppers in Chicago, 1926 (from left to right: Omer Simeon, Andrew Hilaire, John Lindsay, Jelly Roll Morton [in front], Johnny St. Cyr, Kid Ory, George Mitchell).

LOUIS ARMSTRONG

JAZZ'S FIRST SOLO GENIUS

One of the true icons in the history of jazz, Louis Armstrong's contribution cannot be overstated. Prior to his arrival on the scene as the premier cornetist-trumpeter of the mid-1920s, jazz had been primarily an ensemble art form, perhaps best exemplified by New Orleans groups led by such prominent jazz men as trombonist Kid Ory and cornetist King Oliver. Armstrong's revolutionary Hot Five recordings from 1925–1927, the first under his own name, single-handedly altered the course of jazz for all time. His un-precedented facility and creativity during virtuoso solo passages on tunes like "Hotter Than That," "Strut-tin' With Some Barbecue," "Potato Head Blues," "Tight Like This" and "West End Blues" breathed new life into jazz, effectively transforming the music into a soloist's art form.

Later in his distinguished career, Armstrong became an important ambassador for jazz internationally. He toured Europe as early as 1932 and continued traveling abroad with his All-Stars through the 1940s, the 1950s and the 1960s. A remarkably expressive singer as well as a trumpet player and cornetist of un-paralleled virtuosity, Armstrong's loose and improvisational vocal style influenced everyone from Bing Crosby and Connie Boswell to Billie Holiday and Ella Fitzgerald and every singer who followed in their wake. And though Armstrong may have been known in the 1920s for his incendiary hot jazz style, his theme song in later years became "When It's Sleepy Town Down South," a sentimental tune that perfect-ly captured the Big Easy ambiance of his native New Orleans.

Armstrong was born on 4 August 1901, though he and his manager had long insisted that his birthday fell on the symbolic date of 4 July 1900 (the facts were not ascertained until his actual birth certificate was discovered by biographers some years after his death). The grandson of slaves, he spent his youth in poverty. Abandoned by his father and mother, he was raised in the New Orleans Home for Colored Waifs, where he developed his cornet skills. As a teenager, he played in brass bands, took lessons with trum-peter Bunk Johnson and came under the influence of cornetist and bandleader Joe "King" Oliver, who be-came a mentor and father figure to him. Armstrong played on the riverboats in Fate Marable's band and in 1919 he replaced Oliver in Kid Ory's band. By 1922, Armstrong had left New Orleans and traveled to Chica-go, where he had joined Oliver's Creole Jazz Band. He soon became the talk of the Windy City and the dar-ling of hot jazz fans. By 1925, he had begun making his own mark on jazz with his Hot Fives recordings. By 1929, as the center of jazz shifted from Chicago to New York, Armstrong moved with it. He first performed in the pit orchestra for the all-black musical revue *Hot Chocolates*, making a cameo vocal appearance on

Fats Waller's "Ain't Misbehavin'," which later became a hit record for him. He soon followed with a hit version of Hoagy Carmichael's "Stardust" in 1931 and had hits as well with such vocal numbers as "I'm Confessin' (That I Love You)," "Body and Soul," "Black and Blue" and "I Can't Give You Anything But Love." He had effectively transformed himself from a virtuoso instrumental jazz performer to a beloved entertainer who occupied a huge place in the American psyche.

Armstrong's charismatic persona lit up the screen in several movies, beginning with 1936's *Pennies From Heaven* and continuing with 1938's *Dr. Rhythm*, 1941's *Birth of the Blues*, 1943's *Cabin in the Sky* and 1947's *New Orleans* (featuring Billie Holiday). Perhaps his most famous screen role was the 1956 film *High Society*, which included Armstrong exchanging licks with Bing Crosby on the anthemic "Now You Has Jazz." He also scored hit singles in 1956 with a version of "Mack the Knife" (from Kurt Weill's 1928 musical *The Threepenny Opera*) and in 1964 with "Hello Dolly!," theme song for the Broadway musical of the same name which was subsequently made into a movie in 1969 starring Barbra Streisand and featuring Armstrong himself in an on-screen appearance. He died from a heart attack on 6 July 1971, a month before his 70th birthday. His highly sentimental "What a Wonderful World" became a posthumous hit for the jazz legend and has been subsequently used in countless films and television programs over the years.

25 | A young Louis Armstrong in London on his first tour of Europe in 1933. Louis, sporting a herringbone suit and matching cap with argyle socks.

26-27 | Armstrong on the porch of his house in Corona, Queens on 29 June 1970, surrounded by young children from the neighborhood. **27 |** Louis strolling down the street hand-in-hand with his wife Lucille, 1960. **28-29 |** Armstrong at a rehearsal for a session in early 1960 with the Dukes of Dixieland with drumming legend Gene Krupa sitting in on drums.

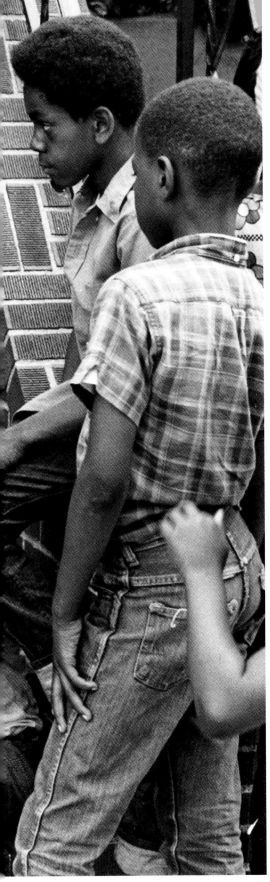

"What we play is life. My whole life, my whole soul, my whole spirit is to play that horn."

Louis Armstrong

"The bottom line of any country
in the world is 'what did we
contribute to the world?'
...We contributed Louis Armstrong."

Tony Bennett

SIDNEY BECHET

STAR SOLOIST OF SOPRANO SAX

The great Creole soprano saxophonist from New Orleans once cautioned against treating jazz like a precious museum artifact. "There's this mood about the music, a kind of need to be moving," he said. "You just can't set it down and hold it. Those Dixieland musicians, they tried to write the music down and kind of freeze it. Even when they didn't arrange it to death, they didn't have any place to send it. That's why they lost it. You just can't keep the music unless you move with it."

Bechet's forceful delivery, powerful tone and distinctive, wide vibrato was always moving. So thrilling were his performances that, while living in Paris, he inspired European critics to regard the blues as high art. The eminent Swiss conductor Ernest Ansermet upheld Bechet as "the highway the whole world will swing along tomorrow." Indeed, Bechet's flights on his chosen instrument inspired John Coltrane to pick up the soprano sax in the mid 1960s.

Born on 14 May 1897, the youngest of seven children, he played with all the greats in New Orleans (Kid Ory, Bunk Johnson, Freddie Keppard, King Oliver, Louis Armstrong). In 1919 he joined Will Marion Cook's Southern Syncopated Orchestra and traveled to London, where they performed at the Royal Philharmonic Hall. During their European tour, Bechet received an ecstatic review from conductor Ansermet: "There is in the Southern Syncopated Orchestra an extraordinary clarinet virtuoso who is, so it seems, the first of his race to have composed perfectly formed blues on the clarinet. I wish to set down the name of this artist of genius. As for myself, I shall never forget it. It is Sidney Bechet." While in London, Bechet discovered the soprano saxophone and it would become his main instrument from then on.

On 30 July 1923, Bechet recorded with Louis Armstrong on sessions for the Clarence Williams Blue Five. He returned to Paris in 1925 to perform with Josephine Baker in the popular "La Revue Negre" at Théâtre des Champs Élysées. Following an altercation at a club involving gun play, Bechet was arrested and spent the next 11 months in a Parisian jail. When he got out, he worked in Berlin for a while before returning to New York in 1929, eventually hooking up with Duke Ellington's orchestra in 1931. Shortly after, he formed his New Orleans Feetwarmers in 1932 and performed at the Savoy Ballroom in Harlem. The group, co-led by New Orleans-bred trumpeter Tommy Ladnier, recorded six joyously swinging sides for the Victor label. Bechet scored a hit in 1939 with a soulful rendition of George Gershwin's "Summertime," accompanied by pianist Meade Lux Lewis and drummer Big Sid Catlett. The

success of that recording essentially saved the fledgling Blue Note label from bankruptcy. On 18 April 1941, as an early experiment in overdubbing at Victor, Bechet recorded a version of the pop song "The Sheik of Araby," playing six different instruments: clarinet, soprano saxophone, tenor saxophone, piano, bass, and drums.

Through the 1940s, Bechet played around Chicago and also appeared on several of Eddie Condon's Town Hall shows in New York. He returned to France in 1949 and by the early 1950s was a major celebrity in Paris and a national hero in France, although by that time he was hardly known at all in his homeland. In 1957, Bechet recorded an excellent record with French bop-inspired pianist Martial Solal. Shortly before his death in Paris on 14 May 1959, his 62nd birthday, Bechet dictated his autobiography, "Treat It Gentle." He was inducted into the *Down Beat* Jazz Hall of Fame in 1968.

34-35 | Bechet strolling by Rue Armstrong and Rue Bechet in Paris, circa 1958.

36-37 | A product of New Orleans, Bechet was a major celebrity in Paris and a national hero in France during the early 1950s.

BIX
BEIDERBECKE

JAZZ AGE TRUMPET PHENOMENON

One of the early jazz tragedies, cornetist Leon Bismark "Bix" Beiderbecke attained cult hero status during the 1920s, only to die from acute alcoholism at age 28. His most famous solos have been dissected note-for-note by generations of trumpeters. And though his career was all too brief, in death his legend has only grown over time.

Born on 23 March 1903 in Davenport, Iowa, Bix rebelled against his strict, late-Victorian upbringing by becoming a cornetist who played hot jazz. He was 15 years old when he came under the spell of "Tiger Rag" and "Dixie Jass Band One Step" by the Original Dixieland Jass Band, the first band to record jazz commercially. Bix began learning the lines of the ODJB's cornetist, Nick LaRocca. And from the outset, he produced a remarkably warm, seductive sound later described by one writer as "sweet hot."

When Beiderbecke's parents sent him away to a boarding school near Chicago, his personal demons began to manifest themselves. Due to his chronic drinking — something of a sport during the years of Prohibition in the United States from 1920 to 1933 — he was expelled from school before the first academic year was over. In 1923, he joined the Wolverines and the following year made his first recordings with the group — "Fidgety Feet" and "Jazz Me Blues." Bix also recorded some stellar sides later in 1924 with the Sioux City Six, featuring C-melody saxophonist Frankie Trumbauer, marking the beginning of a fruitful partnership between Bix and Tram (as he was called). The two soon became figureheads for a generation of young white Chicago musicians trying to play hot jazz, including clarinetists Benny Goodman, Pee Wee Russell and Frank Teschemacher, tenor saxophonist Bud Freeman, cornetist Jimmy McPartland, pianist Joe Sullivan, guitarist Eddie Condon and drummer Gene Krupa. Collectively, they developed the Chicago style, a more raucous, rhythmically aggressive take on traditional New Orleans jazz.

By the time he was 23, Bix was a confirmed alcoholic. But drinking did not appear to interfere with his gift for melodic improvisation. In 1926, Bix and Tram toured widely with the Jean Goldkette Orchestra. During this period, Bix also recorded two masterpieces — "I'm Comin' Virginia" and "Singin' the Blues" — with a small group led by Trumbauer and featuring guitarist Eddie Lang. Trumpeters everywhere quickly set about learning each of his solos on those influential recordings. After the Goldkette outfit disbanded, Bix and Tram both joined the popular Paul Whiteman Orchestra, led by the self-proclaimed "King of Jazz." While Whiteman's group was considered genteel in comparison to the Trumbauer or Goldkette bands, Beiderbecke nevertheless turned in some brief solo gems on tunes like "Mississippi Mud" and "Tain't So" (both featuring a young Bing Crosby). In 1929, his health deteriorating from drinking, Beiderbecke had a nervous breakdown and was sent to a sanitorium in Davenport for rest and rehabilitation. Once back on the scene in New York, he began drinking again and his physical and emotional state went into a rapid decline. Suffering from pneumonia and acute alcoholism, he died alone in a boarding house in Queens on 6 August 1931.

40-41 | Bix Beiderbecke and the Wolverines in the Gennett Studios in Richmond, Indiana, circa 1924.

DUKE ELLINGTON
ELEGANT MAESTRO, JAZZ AMBASSADOR

One of the most famous names in jazz history, second only to Louis Armstrong, Edward Kennedy Ellington (a.k.a. Duke) was the most prolific composer and important bandleader for a span of over 50 years.

The son of a White House butler, Edward Kennedy Ellington was born on 29 April 1899 and grew up in comfortable surroundings in Washington D.C. Beginning piano lessons at age seven, he was writing music by his teens and by 1917 dropped out of high school to pursue a career in music. He was a member of a 5-piece group called The Washingtonians, which relocated to New York in 1923, taking up residency at The Kentucky Club. The group made its first recordings in November 1924 and later came under Ellington's leadership, playing a raucous brand of jazz that was dubbed "jungle style" and featured the growling trumpet work of James "Bubber" Miley. (This era is best represented by their 1927 recording "East St. Louis Toodle-oo"). The Ellington band later took a job uptown at The Cotton Club. Live radio broadcasts from the famed Harlem club during the band's 3-year residency made Ellington a household name.

By 1931, Ellington had scored a hit with an instrumental version of one of his standards, "Mood Indigo" and the following year introduced his anthemic "It Don't Mean a Thing (If It Ain't Got That Swing)," featuring singer Ivie Anderson. He followed with a succession of hits in "Sophisticated Lady," "Solitude" and "Reminiscing in Tempo." In early 1939, a young composer-arranger-pianist from Pittsburgh named Billy Strayhorn joined the organization and became Ellington's composing partner and right-hand man. In the summer of 1941, this edition of the group recorded Strayhorn's "Take the A Train," which became the band's theme song. Ellington's band remained a powerhouse through the 1940s, churning out such hits as "I Got It Bad (And That Ain't Good)," "Don't Get Around Much Anymore," "Do Nothin' Till You Hear from Me" and "I'm Beginning to See the Light." After experiencing something of a decline in the early 1950s, the Ellington band made a major comeback at the 1956 Newport Jazz Festival on the strength of a dazzling performance that featured a long, show-stopping solo by tenor saxophonist Paul Gonsalvez in "Dimuendo and Crescendo in Blue." That historic performance was documented on his first Columbia album, *Ellington at Newport*, the best-selling album of his career.

In 1959, Ellington scored the film *Anatomy of a Murder* and two years later was nominated for an Academy Award for his next score, *Paris Blues*. He recorded the first of his sacred concerts in 1965, winning a Grammy Award for best original jazz composition for "In the Beginning, God." His 1967 album *Far East Suite*, inspired by a tour of the Middle and Far East, won the Best Instrumental Jazz Performance Grammy that year, and he took home his sixth Grammy in the same category in 1969 for *And His Mother Called Him Bill*, his tribute to Strayhorn, who had died in 1967. Ellington followed with such ambitious works as 1971's *New Orleans Suite* and 1972's *Togo Brava Suite*. Ellington continued to perform regularly with his orchestra until he was overcome by illness in the spring of 1974. He died on 24 May 1974 at age 75.

44-45 | Duke Ellington and his Cotton Club Orchestra, early 1930s.

46 | Maestro Ellington at age 68, conducting his orchestra through his *Far East Suite* in 1967. 47 | Duke at the piano in concert at the Fairfield Hall, Croydon during a British tour in 1963.

48-49 | Ellington was one of the most prolific composers and important bandleaders for a span of over 50 years.

50 | Ellington directing his orchestra at the Hammersmith Odeon in London, October 1971.

51 | On the set of "We Love You Madly," a Duke Ellington tribute show filmed in Hollywood on 13 January 1973, just a year before his death.

CAB CALLOWAY

HIS HI-DE-HIGHNESS OF HO-DE-HO

A consummate entertainer, Calloway's unmistakable charisma reached to the very back row at every venue he ever played. His frantic stage moves and wild showmanship during the 1930s laid the groundwork for jivesters from the likes Louis Jordan and Louis Prima to proto-rockers Little Richard and Jerry Lee Lewis and his slick dance moves while conducting his big band (including an early precursor of The Moonwalk) pre-dated Michael Jackson's stage choreography by four decades. A pioneering jivester, Calloway took the seeds planted by Louis Armstrong and Fats Waller in the 1920s and reaped a righteous harvest in the 1930s.

A handsome and dapper man, Calloway became a household name throughout America in 1932 on the strength of his breakthrough hit song, "Minnie the Moocher." He proceeded to marry his playful, good-humored nature to jazz in a string of jive anthems that followed, including "Are You Hep to the Jive?," "Are You All Reet?," "We the Cats Shall Hep Ya" and "Jumpin' Jive." His appearances on radio, in movies (*The Big Broadcast of 1932*, *International House* and *Stormy Weather*) and cartoons of the day (*Betty Boop*, *Jack Frost*) further elevated his profile in the 1930s. And, in 1936, the publication of *Cab Calloway's Hepster's Dictionary* (an annotated glossary of his expansive jive vocabulary) helped to spread the word of jive talk, fanning the flames of this popular fad.

In the early years of the Great Depression, when millions of Americans were out of work, displaced from their farms and wholly dependent on government handouts and food banks, Calloway was earning $50,000 a year and living in high style – wearing the finest clothes, driving a big green Lincoln convertible around town, flashing a smoldering sensuality and attracting throngs of admiring females wherever he went. As Al Quaglieri wrote in his liner notes to the 1994 Columbia Records compilation, *Are You Hep to the Jive?*: "That toothy, worldwise grin…that thin moustache…those lascivious eyes…that tangle of shiny black hair dangling carelessly over his forehead. Since time began, whenever parents warned their daughters about dangerous men, this was the very guy they meant."

Cabell Calloway was born on Christmas Day in 1907 in Rochester, New York. Raised in a middle-class section of Baltimore, he became a star basketball player in high school and had dreams of turning pro but eventually decided on a career in music instead. Inspired by the flamboyant drummer and bandleader Chick Webb, he turned to drums and played briefly in a 10-piece band around Baltimore. After graduating from high school in 1927, he joined an all-male vocal quartet that was featured in a touring production of a black revue called *Plantation Days*. The show eventually traveled to Chicago in September of that year.

In January 1928, Cab began singing at the Dreamland Café, right across the street from the Sunset Café, where Louis Armstrong was the talk of Chicago. By the Spring of 1928, Calloway had become the mc at the Sunset, where he and Armstrong worked together for about six months. Two years later, Armstrong would be responsible for getting Cab his first major gig in New York in the cast of the musical revue, *Hot Chocolates*. "I suppose that Louis was one of the main influences in my career," he wrote in his autobiography, *Of Minnie the Moocher and Me*. "Later on, I began to scat sing with all of that hi-de-ho-ing. Louis first got me freed up from straight lyrics to try scatting."

By November 1929, Calloway was back in New York leading The Alabamians at the Savoy Ballroom in Harlem. The following year he took over leadership of The Missourians, which eventually replaced Duke Ellington's band at The Cotton Club. It was there that Cab developed his dazzling showmanship and slick brand of jive that would launch him to stardom. His 1931 recording of "Minnie the Moocher," with its catchy call-and-response chorus of "hi-de-hi-de-hi-de-ho," made him an overnight sensation. That tune would become Calloway's theme song and he continued to perform it for audiences over the next six decades.

Cab always hired first-rate jazz musicians for his bands. Such stellar instrumentalists as bassist Milt Hinton, guitarist Danny Barker, saxophonist Ben Webster and a precocious young trumpeter named John Birks "Dizzy" Gillespie passed through the ranks of Calloway's bands in the 1930s. His longstanding engagement at The Cotton Club finally ended in 1940 and by 1947 Cab had, reluctantly, broken up his big band and scaled down to a septet he called The Cab Jivers.

In 1950, Calloway opened on Broadway in a revival of the George & Ira Gershwin opera *Porgy and Bess*. He played the role of Sportin' Life opposite opera star Leontyne Price in that production which ran for three and a half years. In 1967, he starred in an all-black production of *Hello Dolly* with Pearl Bailey. A cameo appearance in the popular 1980 film *The Blues Brothers* helped spark renewed interest in this jive pioneer. Cab continued to perform in public well into his 80s before suffering a stroke in May 1994. He died six months later on 18 November.

54-55 | A rare meeting of the minds — Duke Ellington on guitar (flanked by gospel singer and guitarist Rosetta Tharpe and cornetist Rex Stewart) and Cab Calloway on piano during a jam session at a private party hosted by Hearst political cartoonist Burris Jenkins, in his studio, New York City, 1939.

"My audience was my life. What I did and how I did it, was all for my audience."

Cab Calloway

FATS WALLER

EBULLIENT JIVESTER, STRIDE STYLIST

One of the most ebullient and beloved figures in the history of jazz, Thomas Wright "Fats" Waller was a stellar stride pianist and prolific singer-songwriter who delivered such popular jive-oriented ditties as "Hold Tight (I Want Some Seafood, Mama)," "Ain't Misbehavin'," "Honeysuckle Rose," "The Joint Is Jumpin'" and "Your Feets Too Big" with broad strokes of comedic panache. A self-appointed missionary for the cause of letting the good times roll, Waller was also one of the first jazz musicians to take advantage of the medium of film to promote his music via "soundies," short black-and-white films made in the early 1940s that were forerunners of today's music videos and could be viewed for a dime through coin-operated movie jukeboxes at cinemas, nightclubs, restaurants, lounges and amusement centers across the United States. And though today he is regarded as one of jazz's larger-than-life figures, Waller's penchant for entertaining has almost overshadowed his remarkable skills as a pianist.

Born on 21 May 1904, Waller was a precocious child whose pianistic talents emerged at an early age. The son of a preacher at the famous Abyssinian Baptist Church in Harlem, Waller began playing the organ in church. By age 15, he had become something of a sensation around his Harlem neighborhood, known by all of his schoolmates as the house organist at the Lincoln Theater, where he entertained during intermission between movie features. His prodigious Johnson-influenced style, a syncopated derivation of Scott Joplin's ragtime piano style with steady-pumping bass lines in the left hand and dazzling filigrees in the right hand, was first documented at age 18 for Okeh Records. Two songs were recorded in those sessions held in late October 1922 — "Muscle Shoals Blues" and "Birmingham Blues." Shortly thereafter, Waller began collaborating on songwriting with another mentor figure, Clarence Williams, who was an accomplished pianist and leader of the Blue Five recording group. An astute businessman, Williams would help guide Waller's career in the early years.

Another key figure in Waller's career was Andy Razaf, a gifted lyricist from Washington, D.C. who would become Fats' writing partner on a string of tunes from the successful Jazz Age revues *Load of Coal*, *Keep Shufflin'* and *Hot Chocolates* (the latter a 1929 Broadway production which introduced the tune "Ain't Misbehavin'," sung by a young Louis Armstrong). Waller's own unique singing style was animated, involving freewheeling scatting and off-the-cuff asides that offered commentary on the songs as he delivered them. And he imbued all of these exuberant tunes with an equally animated piano style that relied on a bouncing left hand in combination with an uncommonly graceful yet agile right hand (an approach to the keyboard

61 | Stride piano master, prolific songwriter and ebullient entertainer Fats Waller playing in the comfort of his Harlem home.

that influenced such great jazzmen as Count Basie, Teddy Wilson, Art Tatum and Dave Brubeck). The jovial 300-pound Waller showcased his considerable pianistic talents on such instrumental numbers as "Handful of Keys," "Jitterbug Waltz" and "Smashing Thirds."

In 1939, an exceptionally prolific year for Waller, he released a bevy of hit recordings including "Two Sleepy People," "Good for Nothing but Love," "Tea for Two," "Squeeze Me," "Hold Tight," "Your Feets Too Big," "Honeysuckle Rose," and a duet with a teenaged Una Mae Carlisle on "I Can't Give You Anything But Love." By 1940, he was wildly popular in both the U.S. and Europe and by the time he appeared with Lena Horne in the 1943 film, *Stormy Weather*, Fats was a household name just about everywhere. Unfortunately, his years of late-night carousing,

overeating and heavy drinking finally caught up with him near the end of 1943. Waller died on 15 December 1943 of bronchial pneumonia on a train pulling into Union Station in Kansas City, Missouri. His musical legacy lived on in the 1978 Broadway musical revue, *Ain't Misbehavin'*, which ran for 1604 performances and enjoyed a brief revival in 1988.

62-63 | Fats Waller (front center, with cane) poses with bandleader Les Hite (front, in white) and his orchestra along with club owner Frank Sebastian and the Creole Dancing Revue at Frank Sebastian's New Cotton Club, circa 1935, Culver City, California.

63 | Fats Waller poses with members of the Creole Dancing Revue (a.k.a. Frank Sebastian's Cotton Club Cuties) at Frank Sebastian's New Cotton Club, circa 1935, Culver City, California.

DJANGO REINHARDT
EUROPE'S FIRST JAZZ STAR

A brilliant melodic improviser, guitarist Django Reinhardt was the first European musician to have an impact on American jazz music. His dazzling 32 note runs and filigrees with the Quintet of the Hot Club of France, during the early 1930s, sound as amazing and risk-taking today as they did then. Reinhardt's prodigious dexterity is all the more remarkable considering he had the use of only three fingers on his left hand. Born on 23 January 1910 in Liverchies, Belgium, Reinhardt was a descendant of Manouche Gypsies. By age 14, after switching from banjo to guitar, he had begun working regularly in the clubs of Paris. He progressed rapidly on the instrument and by age 17 was acknowledged as one of the best guitarists in the Gypsy community. On 2 November 1928, Django suffered severe burns while rescuing his wife from a fire in their caravan. His left hand was mutilated, paralyzing the two smaller fingers of his fretting hand for the rest of his life. Through daily woodshedding he was able to train himself to use only the thumb and first two fingers of his left hand, eventually gaining staggering facility with his unorthodox technique.

By 1929, Reinhardt had begun investigating the music of Louis Armstrong, Duke Ellington, Fats Waller and jazz guitar pioneer Eddie Lang. By incorporating some of those jazz references on his acoustic Selmer Maccaferri guitar, he created a vibrant, hybrid style that came to be known as 'Gypsy jazz.' By 1933, Reinhardt had begun playing with a young French violinist named Stephane Grappelli, who was also trying to come to terms with American jazz. They formed a group with Louis Vola on bass, Django's brother, Joseph, on rhythm guitar and Roger Chaput on a second rhythm guitar and in December 1934 made their first Quintet of the Hot Club of France recordings — buoyant renditions of "Dinah" and "Tiger Rag." An instant hit in Europe, they followed up, in 1935, with recordings of Swing era staples like "Avalon," "Limehouse Blues," "Nagasaki," "Honeysuckle Rose" and "Sweet Georgia Brown." By 1937, the cross-fertilization was fully realized through the Quintet of the Hot Club of France collaborations with such American jazz stars as Louis Armstrong, Coleman Hawkins, Benny Carter, Dicky Wells and Rex Stewart.

The outbreak of World War II in 1939 caused the Quintet of the Hot Club of France to disband. Grappelli took up residence in London while Reinhardt remained in Paris and continued to roam Europe, playing with a new quintet featuring clarinetist Hubert Rostaing in place of Grappelli. He toured the U.S. in 1946, playing electric guitar with the Duke Ellington Orchestra and continued playing throughout Europe until his death from a stroke, at age 43, on 16 May 1953. Django's most popular compositions — "Minor Swing," "Daphne," "Belleville," "Djangology," "Swing '42" and "Nuages" — have become jazz standards.

65 | Gypsy jazz guitar virtuoso Django Reinhardt, photographed on 1 January 1940.

COUNT BASIE

SWINGING THE BLUES

There are precious few elite musicians in jazz who have been accorded regal status via their nicknames — Joe "King" Oliver, Edward "Duke" Ellington and William "Count" Basie immediately come to mind. All were beloved, larger-than-life figures, but Basie was, perhaps, most closely associated with the straight ahead 4/4 swing pulse that came to define jazz during the Swing Era. And he presided with regal authority over his dynamic riff-based big band for nearly 50 years.

The heart of Basie's well-oiled machine was its supple, swinging rhythm section. From its inception in 1937, that tightly-knit unit consisted of bassist Walter Page, drummer Jo Jones, guitarist Freddie Green and Basie himself on piano. This is the lineup that propelled such classic Basie numbers as "Swinging the Blues," "One O'Clock Jump," "Lester Leaps In" and "Jumpin' at the Woodside" while the spotlight shone on such star soloists as tenor saxophonists Lester Young and Herschel Evans, trombonist Dicky Wells and trumpeter Buck Clayton. Subsequent rhythm sections would provide that same swinging momentum for such potent soloists as tenor saxophonists Don Byas, Buddy Tate, Lucky Thompson, Illinois Jacquet, Eddie "Lockjaw" Davis, Ernie Wilkins, Frank Wess and Frank Foster, trumpeters Harry "Sweets" Edison, Snooky Young and Thad Jones and trombonists Al Grey and Benny Powell. At the core of all these cohesive aggregations was Basie's spare yet exuberant piano style, marked by his economical choice of notes and a few "plink plink" interjections along with occasional stride passages.

A native of Red Bank, New Jersey, Basie was born on 21 August 1904. As a teenager, he played piano for silent films shown at the local Red Bank cinema and by age 19 he had begun hanging out in Harlem, where he received tips from stride piano master Fats Waller. His first road experience came while accompanying performers on the vaudeville circuit. In 1927, he found himself stuck in Kansas City when the troupe he was traveling with disbanded. In 1928, he joined Walter Page's Blue Devils, which featured trumpeter Oran "Hot Lips" Page and singer Jimmy Rushing. After a year, he left the Blue Devils to join Bennie Moten's territory band. Following Moten's untimely death in 1935, Basie took over the 9-piece band, which he originally called the Barons of Rhythm. High-profile gigs at The Grand Terrace in Chicago and the Roseland Ballroom in New York led to a recording contract with Decca Records in 1937. Their recording of "One O'Clock Jump" later that year was the band's first chart-topper and ultimately became the Count Basie Orchestra theme song for the next half century.

67 | Count Basie leading his orchestra in concert in Manchester, England, circa 1957.

The mid 1950s marked the emergence of the so-called new testament band, which featured more modern, streamlined arrangements by Neal Hefti, Frank Foster, Thad Jones and Frank Wess. Vocalist Joe Williams was introduced on 1956's *Count Basie Swings, Joe Williams Sings*, which included the hit single, "Every Day (I Have the Blues)." Other Basie classics from this period include "April in Paris," "Corner Pocket" and "Shiny Stockings," along with the elegant and alluring "Lil' Darlin'." Basie recorded several all-star small group sessions during the 1970s for Norman Granz's Pablo label. He continued touring with his big band through the early 1980s and died of pancreatic cancer on 26 April 1984 at age 79. His legacy has been carried on by tribute bands led in succession by Basie alumni Thad Jones, Frank Foster, Grover Mitchell and Bill Hughes.

68-69 | Count Basie leading a 1942 jam session with members of his band, including Lester Young (far left, with pork pie hat) at the studio of *Life* magazine photographer Gjon Mili.

69 | Duke Ellington and Count Basie during sessions for the Columbia Records album *First Time!*, July 1961.

CHICK WEBB

SULTAN OF THE SAVOY BALLROOM

A hunch-backed drummer who led the house band at the Savoy Ballroom during the height of the Swing era, William "Chick" Webb was a strict taskmaster who drove his outfit with a crisp, aggressive style from behind the kit. At its peak, the Chick Webb Orchestra was on a par with popular outfits like the Count Basie Orchestra and the Benny Goodman Orchestra, often going toe-to-toe with them in the "Battle of the Bands" at the Savoy. Webb was also noted for having discovered teenaged vocalist Ella Fitzgerald, who joined his band in 1935 and eventually took over leadership of the outfit when he died in 1939.

Born on 10 February 1905 in Baltimore, Webb suffered from congenital tuberculosis as an infant, which left him short of stature and with a badly deformed spine. Because of his ill health and poor upbringing, he had received virtually no formal schooling. Webb began playing drums at an early age and first played professionally at age 11. By age 17 he had moved to New York and within two years was leading his own band in Harlem. Through the 1920s, Webb toured with his band while also having extended engagements in New York clubs.

In 1931, the Chick Webb Orchestra became the house band at the Savoy Ballroom, where he helped usher in the new "Swing" era with his crisp, aggressive style and prodigious technique on the kit along with his relentlessly competitive spirit. A champion of the drums and a born showman, Webb performed with his drums perched high upon a platform. He used custom-made pedals, a big, 28-inch, bass drum and a wide variety of other percussion instruments to create his thundering, show-stopping solos. Drummer Buddy Rich cited Webb as a significant influence, calling him "the daddy of them all." Drummer-bandleaders Art Blakey, Gene Krupa and Louie Bellson also credited Webb with influencing their music. As Swing era drummer Cozy Cole explained to jazz writer Dan Morgenstern: "We'd all come to the Savoy Ballroom and stand around Chick and it seemed the more drummers that were around, the better he'd play. He had a beautiful conception and a great band. He inspired us all."

During Webb's tenure at the Savoy Ballroom, such great musicians as saxophonists Benny Carter and Johnny Hodges and pioneering jump blues star Louis Jordan passed through the ranks of his band. On 12 May 1937, Webb's Orchestra participated in an historic "Battle of the Bands" with the Benny Goodman Orchestra. By all accounts, Chick's group triumphed that night. The following year, Webb scored his biggest hit with "A-Tisket A-Tasket," sung with girlish delight by a young Ella.

71 | The dynamic drummer and showman Chick Webb leading his powerhouse orchestra from behind the drum kit, early 1930s.

BENNY GOODMAN

THE KING OF SWING

A clarinet virtuoso, a brilliant improviser and, by all accounts, a demanding bandleader, Benny Goodman helped move jazz into the mainstream during the so-called Swing Era (1935–1946). With his big band, trio, quartet and sextet, Goodman appealed to dancers and jazz aficionados alike, and, particularly, to the college crowd. During an era of segregation, Goodman pioneered race relations from the bandstand. His 1936 quartet, which included black musicians Teddy Wilson on piano and Lionel Hampton on vibraphone, alongside white drummer Gene Krupa, was among the first racially-integrated jazz groups to record and play together. As Goodman once said, "I'm selling music, not prejudice." And as Hampton noted, years later, "As far as I'm concerned, what Benny did in those days made it possible for Negroes to have their chance in baseball and other fields."

Goodman was also savvy enough to hire gifted black arrangers, like Fletcher Henderson and Edgar Sampson, to provide their swinging, syncopated touch to current pop tunes like "King Porter Stomp," "Runnin' Wild," "Avalon," "Moonglow," "Bugle Call Rag," "Memories of You" and the popular Yiddish tune of the day, "Bei Mir Bistu Shein." Following Goodman's initial burst of popularity, which began in 1935, swing bands sprang up like mushrooms. By 1937, there were dozens of swing bands playing to huge crowds across the country. By 1939, there were hundreds of them. And, during this prosperous era for big bands, like those led by Tommy and Jimmy Dorsey, Glenn Miller, Artie Shaw, Charlie Barnet, Woody Herman and others, Goodman reigned as "The King of Swing."

Born on 30 May 1909, in Chicago, Goodman began studying the clarinet at age 10. Influenced by the great New Orleans clarinetists Jimmy Noone, Johnny Dodds and Leon Rappolo, as well as by the eccentric Dixieland style of Pee Wee Russell, he developed quickly and quit school at age 14 to start gigging around Chicago. At age 16, he was hired by the Ben Pollack band and later moved to Los Angeles. In 1929, Goodman left Pollack's band and moved to New York, where he played on recording sessions and radio shows. He formed his first band in 1934 and, later that year, won a spot on NBC's weekly radio show "Let's Dance," which instantly elevated his profile and led to a recording contract and a national tour in 1935. A breakthrough performance at the Palomar Ballroom in Los Angeles that year made Goodman a household name.

One of Goodman's immediate competitors during the early years of the Swing Era was drummer Chick Webb, who led an all-black big band that had a longstanding residency at the Savoy Ballroom in Harlem.

73 | Benny Goodman, the "King of Swing," wielding a
mean clarinet, mid 1930s.

74 | Benny Goodman
exciting a crowd of young
swing band enthusiasts
at the Palomar Ballroom
in Los Angeles, circa
1935.

75 | Benny Goodman and
his horn section on the
set of the 1943 motion
picture, "The Gang's All
Here."

The two bands engaged in a celebrated duel at the Savoy on 11 May 1937 billed as "The Music Battle of the Century." By some published accounts, Webb's band (which also featured a young singer
named Ella Fitzgerald) won the battle. The following year, Goodman's legend grew following his appearance at the historic 1938 concert at Carnegie Hall, which, symbolically, was jazz's 'coming out'
party into the world of 'respectable' music. That groundbreaking concert, on 16 January, climaxed
with a rousing rendition of Louis Prima's "Sing, Sing, Sing," a drum feature for Krupa that brought
greater visibility for the drummer and resulted in him forming his own big band later that year.

At the height of his popularity, Goodman's band appeared in several films including *The Big Broadcast of 1937*, *Stage Door Canteen* (1943) and *Sweet and Lowdown* (1944). By 1946, most of the big
bands had broken up as the Swing Era gave way to the advent of bebop and the popularity of small-
group jazz. A 1955 Hollywood biography on Goodman's life, starring comedian Steve Allen, exposed
a whole new audience to the clarinetist's music. He continued to tour and record in small-group settings through the 1960s and the 1970s and remained active until his death from a heart attack, at
age 77, on 13 June 1986.

76 | Goodman recording at Universal Studios with tenor sax star Stan Getz, 1955.
77 | The King of Swing, taking a scale and making it wail.

"After you've done all the work and prepared as much as you can, what the hell, you might as well go out and have a good time."

Benny Goodman

78-79 | Road warrior Goodman relaxing in his hotel room after a gig, 9 October 1976.

CHARLIE CHRISTIAN
ELECTRIC GUITAR PIONEER

One of the pioneers of the electric guitar, Charlie Christian emerged as a vital new voice in jazz in the early 1940s through his forcefully swinging solos with the Benny Goodman Sextet and Orchestra. His hard driving, horn-like, single-note lines influenced a generation of jazz guitarists, from Herb Ellis and Barney Kessel to George Barnes, Tiny Grimes, Mary Osborne, Les Paul, Tal Farlow, Sal Salvador and Wes Montgomery. Blues guitar giants B.B. King and T-Bone Walker also cite Christian as an important influence.

Born on 29 July 1916 in Bonham, Texas, Christian grew up in Oklahoma City. He began playing the trumpet before switching to the guitar at age 12. Emulating the lines of Count Basie's tenor sax great Lester Young, he developed quickly and by 1934, at age 15, he was playing professionally with Alphonso Trent's territory band. Christian later toured the Southwest with the Anna Mae Winburn Orchestra and by 1937 was playing electric guitar in his own combo in Oklahoma City. After a tip from pianist Mary Lou Williams, who had heard Christian play in Oklahoma City, talent scout John Hammond traveled to Oklahoma City to check out the young guitar talent at the Ritz Cafe. Duly impressed, he later persuaded Benny Goodman to fly Christian to Los Angeles for an audition on 16 August 1939. The guitarist made his recording debut with the Benny Goodman Sextet on 2 October 1939, performing "Rose Room" with vibist Lionel Hampton, pianist Fletcher Henderson, bassist Artie Bernstein and drummer Nick Fatool. Subsequently, he recorded such popular numbers as "Seven Come Eleven," "Flying Home," "Air Mail Special" and "Breakfast Feud" with the Goodman Sextet.

By mid 1940, Christian had begun jamming at the Minton's in Harlem with other like-minded young cutting-edge musicians including Dizzy Gillespie, Thelonious Monk and Kenny Clarke. No one called it 'be-bop' at the time, but they were clearly exploring new musical territory, in those freewheeling uptown jam sessions, that was a precursor to Gillespie and Charlie Parker's revolutionary sounds to come. In February 1941, Christian participated in an all-star session for Blue Note Records with clarinetist Edmund Hall, bassist Israel Crosby and boogie-woogie pianist Meade Lux Lewis on celeste. On 19 February 1941 , he went into the studio with the Goodman Orchestra and recorded the anthemic "Solo Flight," a jazz guitar feature for the ages.

By Spring 1941, Christian had contracted tuberculosis and spent some time in Seaview, a New York City-operated sanitarium on Staten Island, to convalesce. By early 1942, he had come down with a bout of pneumonia. Christian died on 2 March 1942 at age 23. It's amazing how much he accomplished in such a short time. In less than two years, from August 1939 to June 1941, Christian opened a new door for jazz guitarists.

LIONEL HAMPTON

JAMMER
JIVESTER
PIONEERING
VIBIST

A bona fide giant of jazz, vibraphonist-drummer Lionel Hampton was a product of the 1930s Swing Era who went on to lead his own big bands through the 1940s and the 1950s. His lively brand of jump blues, particularly on popular tunes like his 1944 hit "Flying Home" and 1946's "Hey! Ba-Ba-Re-Bop," served as a precursor to rock and roll. An inveterate jammer and beloved figure in jazz, the naturally ebullient Hampton was known for his exuberant showmanship and endless energy in concert. His pioneering work on the vibraphones — he was the first jazz musician to record on the instrument in 1930 as a member of the Les Hite band for a Louis Armstrong session — opened the door for such great vibes players as Red Norvo, Cal Tjader and Milt Jackson.

Hampton (or 'Gates', as he was known to friends and colleagues) also doubled on drums, which he played furiously in exciting drum battles on stage to climax his concerts. But along with his frenetic stage persona — mouth agape, mallets flying, sweat pouring from his brow — he was regarded as a first-rate improviser and lifelong champion for the art of swinging.

Born in Louisville, Kentucky on 20 April 1908, Hampton spent his early childhood in Kenosha, Wisconsin before his family moved to Chicago when he was eight years old. He took xylophone lessons as a teenager and also played drums. After moving to California in 1927, he began playing drums for the Dixieland Blues-Blowers and later joined the Les Hite band at Sebastian's Cotton Club, where he began focusing on vibraphone. After developing into an accomplished vibraphonist, Hampton was hired by Benny Goodman in 1936 as the fourth member of his quartet, which had previously been a trio with drummer Gene Krupa and pianist Teddy Wilson. In an era of racial segregation, Goodman's integrated quartet was a complete anomaly, setting a new precedent in jazz. Hampton continued to perform and record with Goodman's quartet, sextet and big band through 1940, when he formed his own big band. He scored hits with two different versions of his theme song, "Flying Home" — first in 1942 with a honking tenor sax solo by Illinois Jacquet and the second in 1944 with a similarly robust solo by Texas tenor man Arnett Cobb. Hampton's jump blues number "Hey! Ba-Ba-Re-Bop" also rose to the top of the R&B charts in 1946. A veritable Who's Who in Jazz passed through the ranks of Hampton's bands through the 1950s and the 1960s, including bassist Charles Mingus, guitarist Wes Montgomery, vocalists Dinah Washington and Betty Carter, trumpeters Dizzy Gillespie, Cat Anderson, Kenny Dorham and Snooky Young, trombonist Jimmy Cleveland and saxophonists Johnny Griffin and Jerome Richardson. During that period, Hampton also had successful collaborations with pianist Oscar Peterson, tenor saxophonist Stan Getz and trombonist Al Grey.

Hampton continued touring with his band through the 1970s and the 1980s. He was eventually sidelined by a stroke in 1991 and died at age 94 from congestive heart failure on 31 August 2002 in New York City.

84 | Fans congregate outside the New Million Dollar theater in downtown Los Angeles during the peak of Lionel Hampton's popularity in the wake of his 1942 hit, "Flying Home."
85 | A consummate showman, Hampton would invariably leave his vibes and jump on the drum set during his concerts to engage in a rousing solo, replete with flashy, acrobatic stick work.

86-87 | Hampton hamming it up with a pair of wooden spoons in the kitchen at Maxim's restaurant in Nice, France, with chef Jacques Maxim joining in the jam on 'cymbals'.

GENE KRUPA

FLAMBOYANT DRUMMIN' MAN

The first superstar drummer of jazz, Gene Krupa was a champion for the drums throughout his long and illustrious career, which lasted five decades. A flamboyant, energetic figure on the bandstand, he gained fame with the Benny Goodman Orchestra through the 1930s (his dramatic tom tom solo on "Sing, Sing, Sing" from Goodman's famous Carnegie Hall concert of 1938 remains a textbook example of show-stopping pyrotechnics on the kit). Krupa subsequently became a bandleader in his own right and racked up hits during the 1940s with his Gene Krupa Orchestra, which featured singer Anita O'Day and trumpet star Roy Eldridge. His colorful life story, including his marijuana bust in 1943, was portrayed in the 1959 film, *The Gene Krupa Story*, starring Sal Mineo.

Born in Chicago on 15 January 1909, Krupa was the youngest of nine children born to Polish immigrants. While his father wanted Gene to join the priesthood, the young man's fancy turned to music. He started out on saxophone in grade school and switched to drums at age 11, forming his first band the following year. In high school, he befriended a group of like-minded young Chicagoans and New Orleans jazz fans known as the "Austin High Gang," whose ranks included cornetist Jimmy McPartland, bassist Jimmy Lanigan, tenor saxophonist Bud Freeman and clarinetist Frank Teschemacher. Together they recorded four tunes in 1927 with a band under the leadership of banjoist Eddie Condon and Red McKenzie (one of the only comb players in jazz). Krupa's biggest drumming influences during this time were Zutty Singleton, who was playing in Chicago with Louis Armstrong at the time, and New Orleans icon Baby Dodds, a key figure in Joe "King" Oliver's Creole Jazz Band of the early 1920s.

Krupa moved to New York in 1929 and worked with bandleader Red Nichols. By 1933, he had joined Benny Goodman's trio (with pianist Teddy Wilson), the first popular integrated musical group in the United States. The following year his drumming became an important part of Goodman's big band, where his featured drum work made him a national celebrity. On 16 January 1938, as part of producer-promoter John Hammond's "Spirituals to Swing" concert, Goodman's band with Krupa became the first jazz act to play New York's Carnegie Hall. Six weeks later, Krupa left Goodman to form his own orchestra with strings. He scored hits in 1941 and 1942 with "Let Me Off Uptown" and "Thanks for the Boogie Ride," both featuring the vivacious vocals of Anita O'Day.

In the summer of 1943, Krupa was arrested in San Francisco and charged with possession of marijuana. He was sentenced to 90 days and served 84 days. After getting out of jail, Krupa reformed his big

89 | Drummer Gene Krupa, a key sideman in Benny Goodman's small groups and big band during the 1930s and a bandleader of his own popular big band during the 1940s, unleashes on the kit.

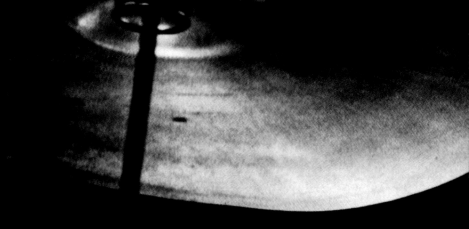

perating, he continued to perform and record with a quartet until finally retiring in 1967, proclaiming, "I feel too lousy to play and I know I must sound lousy." Krupa came out of retirement in 1972 to record with banjoist-guitarist Eddie Condon and trumpeter Wild Bill Davison. His final public performance was a reunion of the old Benny Goodman Quartet on 18 August 1973. He died of leukemia and heart failure two months later on 16 October.

90-91 | A champion of drums throughout his career, Krupa is seen in this 1950 photo playing with wild abandon during one of Norman Granz's Jazz at the Philharmonic concerts.

BILLIE HOLIDAY

LADY SINGS THE BLUES

One of the greatest jazz singers of all time, Billie Holiday possessed an uncanny gift for imbuing a lyric with deep feeling, or underscoring it with meaning, through a myriad of subtle inflections in her inventive phrasing. Swing era trumpeter Roy Eldridge once said of her, "Billie must have come from another world because nobody had the effect on people she had. She could really get to people. I've seen her make them cry and make them happy."

Nicknamed "Lady Day" by tenor sax great Lester Young, she was born Eleanora Fagan on 7 April 1915 in Philadelphia and had a rough life as a child growing up in Baltimore. Her mother, Sadie Fagan, was only 13 when Billie was born and her 15-year-old guitarist-father, Clarence Holiday, abandoned the family. Sexually molested at age 11, she was sent away to a Catholic reform school after being accused of seducing her would-be rapist. After dropping out of school at the fifth grade, she began running errands for the proprietor of a local whorehouse, where she first heard the records of Bessie Smith and Louis Armstrong, her main singing inspirations. Relocating to New York in 1929, she began working in a house of prostitution in Harlem. The house was raided by police and Eleanora spent six months in jail. Upon her release, she began singing in clubs around Harlem, taking the stage name Billie Holiday.

Her big break came after being discovered by talent scout and Columbia Records producer John Hammond. As he told jazz critic Nat Hentoff, "I first heard Billie in early 1933 in a club uptown. She was 17 and she had been scarred by life already. She was going around the tables, singing. And I couldn't believe my ears. She was the first girl singer I'd come across who actually sang like an improvising jazz genius – an extension, almost, of Louis Armstrong. The way she sang around a melody, her uncanny harmonic sense and her sense of lyric content were almost unbelievable in a girl of 17."

Hammond persuaded Benny Goodman to use Holiday on two songs with his orchestra on a November 1933 session, "Your Mother's Son-In-Law" and "Riffin' the Scotch." She later established her reputation with a 1935 Teddy Wilson Orchestra recording of "What A Little Moonlight Can Do," one of her signature tunes in later years. She began recording under her own name in 1936 for the Okeh, Vocalion and Brunswick labels. A two-year engagement at Café Society, Barney Josephson's integrated nightclub in Greenwich Village, made Holiday the talk of the town. It was there that she introduced the somber "Strange Fruit," a protest song based on a poem about the lynching of black men in the South. She recorded the controversial tune for Commodore Records on 20 April 1939 and it remained in her repertoire for the next 20 years. Holiday had

93 | Regal jazz vocalist Billie Holiday, nicknamed Lady Day by tenor sax great Lester Young, had a gift for conveying deep feeling through her inventive phrasing and emotional delivery.

94 | Billie Holiday, seen here in a 1950 performance, was still imbuing her lyrics with a dramatic, heart-wrenching quality toward the end of her career.

95 | Lady Day in mid-1940s form, delivering one of her signature laments, "Good Morning Heartache."

96-97 | Lady Day in the autumn of her years, performing at a 1954 concert, just five years before her death in 1959.

subsequent successes on Commodore with powerfully emotive numbers like "I Cover The Waterfront," "My Old Flame," "I'll Be Seeing You" and her hit song from 1941, "God Bless The Child." She scored similar successes for Decca in the mid 1940s with torch songs like "Lover Man (Oh, Where Can You Be?)," "Don't Explain" and "Good Morning Heartache."

By the 1950s, with her health deteriorating, Holiday's voice grew coarse, reflecting the pain she had endured over a lifetime of abuse, heroin addiction and racism. On 8 December 1957, she gave a profoundly moving performance of her world-weary blues "Fine and Mellow" on the nationally broadcast CBS-TV show, "The Sound of Jazz." Her final recordings in 1958 and 1959 were sad affairs. And though her croaking voice was almost unbearable to hear, it was still imbued with the dramatic, heart-wrenching quality that had made her so special. Suffering from liver and heart disease, she died in hospital on 17 July 1959.

"I hate straight singing. I have to change a tune to my own way of doing it. That's all I know."

Billie Holiday

COLEMAN HAWKINS

THE SONG OF THE HAWK

While the trumpet may have dominated jazz in the early 1920s (via King Oliver, Louis Armstrong, Bix Beiderbecke), the saxophone came to prominence by the end of the decade, spearheaded by the great tenor man Coleman Hawkins. His robust tone and formidable command of chords and harmonies created a benchmark for tenor players through the 1930s.

Born in St. Joseph, Missouri on 21 November 1904, he began playing the piano and switched to tenor sax at age nine. In 1921, he joined blues singer Mamie Smith and her touring group, the Jazz Hounds. At a gig with the Hounds in New York in 1923, he came to the attention of bandleader Fletcher Henderson, who began using Hawkins on recordings that year. During Louis Armstrong's tenure with the band, 1924–1925, Hawkins' playing changed significantly. He became a star soloist with Henderson's band and remained for 11 years. In 1929, Hawkins also participated in one of the earliest integrated recording sessions with Red McKenzie's Mound City Blue Blowers, cutting his first classic ballad statement on "One Hour."

Hawkins left Henderson's band in 1934 to accept an invitation abroad from British bandleader Jack Hylton. He remained in Europe for five years and, in 1937, recorded with Django Reinhardt and Benny Carter in Paris. He returned to the States in 1939 and, shortly after, recorded his masterpiece, "Body and Soul," which further solidified his place as "King of Saxophone" and established him as the most important jazz player of his day. Hawkins made the transition to a more modern style of jazz, participating in the first bebop recording on 16 February 1944 with such younger players as trumpeter Dizzy Gillespie, saxophonists Leo Parker and Don Byas, bassist Oscar Pettiford and drummer Max Roach.

Hawkins continued to record and work regularly both in the United States and in Europe through the 1940s. He recorded another signature tune, "Stuffy," in 1945 and in 1948 recorded the unique, unaccompanied, five-minute performance, "Picasso." Hawkins was a featured soloist on several of Norman Granz's Jazz at the Philharmonic tours in the 1950s. On 8 December 1957, he appeared with Billie Holiday, Coleman Hawkins, Ben Webster, Roy Eldridge and Gerry Mulligan on the nationally broadcast CBS television special, "The Sound of Jazz," performing Holiday's mournful blues, "Fine and Mellow." In 1960, Hawkins played on Max Roach's provocative We Insist! - Freedom Now Suite and in 1962 he participated in the historic Duke Ellington Meets Coleman Hawkins on the Impulse label. The ever-evolving elder then joined with tenor titan Sonny Rollins for a series of encounters in 1963, including Sonny Meets Hawk! and All the Things You Are. He made his last recording in 1966 and died of pneumonia and liver disease on 19 May 1969.

99 | Coleman Hawkins (a.k.a The Hawk), regarded as the Father of Tenor Saxophone, is also renowned for his famous 1939 rendition of "Body and Soul."

LESTER YOUNG

Everything about jazz giant Lester Willis Young was unique. He read comic books, drank buttermilk with whiskey and ate sardines with ice cream. He had protruding, heavy-lidded eyes, a slightly Oriental face, a thin mustache and a snaggle-toothed smile. His walk was light and pigeon-toed and he always wore moccasins or slippers. He wore ankle-length coats and porkpie hats pulled down low and evenly. But more importantly, he introduced a new sensibility to jazz. At a time when Coleman Hawkins' heavier, robust tenor sax tone and aggressive attack was the dominant sound on the scene, Young came along with a cooler, softer tone and melodic invention to chart a different course for the instrument. Nicknamed "Prez" by singer and collaborator Billie Holiday (an abbreviation for President), he was one of the most influential players of his instrument. His inventive, swinging and speech-like lines also profoundly influenced the work of pioneering guitarist Charlie Christian.

Like jivesters Cab Calloway and Slim Gaillard before him, the quintessential hipster Young created an entire lexicon of Lester-speak that was at once bewildering and intriguing. As pianist Horace Silver, who worked with the tenor sax great in 1952, put it: "He had a funny way of saying everything and you really had to learn his language in order to understand what he was saying. For instance, on the bandstand whenever he wanted the bass player to take a solo he would look over at him and say, 'Put me in the basement.' And the cat would start playing the bass solo. Then if Lester wanted him to continue playing another chorus he would say, 'Don't quit now, take another helping.' He had some colorful lingo all his own." Drummer Roy Haynes recalls the day in 1947 when Young invited him to join his band. "He didn't just come out and say, 'Do you want to join my band?' Instead he said, 'Do you have eyes for the slave?' That's the way he expressed it. He was always creative with words that way."

Critic Leonard Feather once wrote of Young: "Prez used an almost entirely personal language that's become standard jazz argot." For instance, 'Bells!' and 'Ding-Dong' signified approval while 'No eyes' indicated reluctance. 'I feel a draft' code for racial discomfort and white musicians were 'gray boys.' In Lesterese, 'Bing and Bob' were the police, a 'hat' was a woman and a 'needle dancer' a heroin addict. 'To be bruised' was to fail and 'Can Madame burn?" meant 'Is your wife a good cook?'"

Regarding his horn work, Young was in a class by himself. As critic Whitney Balliet noted, "He had an airy, lissome tone and an elusive, lyrical way of phrasing that had never been heard before."

Born on 27 August 1909 in Woodville, Mississippi, Young grew up in a musical family. His father was a

multi-instrumentalist who had played in traveling minstrel shows before heading up his own family's band. Lester began playing drums in the family band (which included his brother Lee and sister Irma) at age 10 and toured with them for five years, switching to alto sax at age 13. By the time he had turned 18, Young had fled the family band and joined a Kansas-based group. During the early 1930s he played alto sax with Bennie Moten's territory band, King Oliver's Creole Jazz Band and Walter Page's Blue Devils. After settling in Kansas City in 1933, he acquired his first tenor saxophone and began his first stint with Count Basie's band in 1934. Following brief associations with the Fletcher Henderson and Andy Kirk bands, Young returned to Basie's outfit in 1936 and began his rise to prominence, recording such familiar tunes as "Tickle Toe," "Oh, Lady Be Good," "Shoe Shine Boy," "Taxi War Dance," "Clap Hands, Here Comes Charlie" and his signature piece, "Lester Leaps In."

Young left the Basie band in late 1940. During this period he accompanied singer Billie Holiday on a couple of studio sessions and also made a small set of recordings with Nat "King" Cole in June 1942. He returned to the Basie band in December 1943 and remained for a 10-month stint, until he was drafted into the Army. After being found with marijuana and alcohol among his possessions, Young was court-martialed, served one year in a detention barracks and was dishonorably discharged in late 1945. He returned to the jazz world in 1946, signing on for several tours with Norman Granz's Jazz at the Philharmonic (including one historic 1949 JATP concert at Carnegie Hall with Charlie Parker and Roy Eldridge). Young made a number of studio recordings under Granz's supervision for his Verve Records label during the late 1940s and early 1950s, including more trio recordings with Nat "King" Cole and Buddy Rich as well as sessions with pianists Oscar Peterson and Teddy Wilson. He also recorded extensively for Aladdin Records and Savoy during this period.

By the mid 1950s, Young's health was in serious decline because of his excessive drinking. He was hospitalized in 1955 following a nervous breakdown and emerged in 1956 with a new lease on life, touring Europe with Miles Davis and the Modern Jazz Quartet. In 1957, he had a celebrated reunion with the Count Basie Orchestra at George Wein's Newport Jazz Festival and in December of that year he appeared with Billie Holiday, Coleman Hawkins, Ben Webster, Roy Eldridge and Gerry Mulligan on the CBS television special *The Sound of Jazz*, performing brilliantly on Holiday's tunes "Lady Sings The Blues" and "Fine and Mellow." But it was also clear from this TV broadcast (he was the only horn player seated during the performance) that Young was gravely ill.

Suffering from liver disease and malnutrition, his playing was significantly diminished in the final two years of his life. Young's last studio recordings and live performances came in Paris in March 1959 with drummer Kenny Clarke. Back in New York, he drank himself to death in his room at the Alvin Hotel, just across the street from Birdland. He died in the early hours of the morning on 15 March 1959 at age 49. His longtime friend Billie Holiday died four months later at age 44.

CHARLIE PARKER

HIGH-FLYING BIRD AND THE BIRTH OF BEBOP

A heroic, Dionysian figure in the history of jazz and an inspiration to generations of musicians, alto saxophonist Charlie Parker blazed a new modern trail that sparked the bebop movement. His startling virtuosity on such daunting bop showpieces as "KoKo," "Groovin' High" and "Salt Peanuts" revolutionized jazz in the mid 1940s, pointing toward the future and away from the Swing era that had preceded him. Parker's unprecedented mastery of his horn, along with his tremendously fertile imagination as an improviser, set a new standard on the instrument for the legion of players who followed in his wake, including Sonny Stitt, Phil Woods, Jimmy Heath, Lou Donaldson, Cannonball Adderley, Jackie McLean, Eric Dolphy and others.

Rather than being a reaction against Swing era sax styles, Parker's volatile approach was an organic evolution from Swing. Indeed, he was hugely influenced by Count Basie's tenor star Lester Young and he built on that swinging foundation to create a new vocabulary of musical phrases and methods of improvisation that still resonates with power and relevance today. Parker's innovations from over 60 years ago — new ways of selecting notes against chords, accenting notes to maximize syncopation, expanding harmony by implying passing chords and nonchalantly interspersing solos with double-time and quadruple-time figures — have been fully absorbed by modern day alto stars like Kenny Garrett, Vincent Herring, Steve Coleman and Greg Osby.

Born on 29 August 1920 in Kansas City, Kansas, Parker dropped out of school at age 15 to become a fulltime jazz musician. By that time, he had also acquired the heroin habit that would plague him for the rest of his life. By age 19, Parker had moved to New York and got a job washing dishes at Jimmy's Chicken Shack, where he heard piano great Art Tatum play every night. After returning to Kansas City in 1940 for his father's funeral, he joined pianist Jay McShann's territory band, where he learned on the bandstand from veteran altoist Buster Smith. Parker made his first recordings with McShann's orchestra in 1941 ("Hootie Blues," "Swingmatism") and by December, 1942 he had joined the Earl Hines Orchestra, where he forged a friendship with trumpeter Dizzy Gillespie.

When not gigging with Hines, they would conduct musical experiments, after hours, at Minton's Playhouse in Harlem. The two kindred spirits had a brief stint in Billy Eckstine's band in 1944 and by the end of the year were leading their own bands on fabled 52nd Street. Now famously called Bird (an abbreviation of Yardbird, slang for chicken — his favorite fried food), Parker's quasi-legendary status grew in the mid 1940s. And yet, the ill effects of heroin and alcohol abuse began to manifest themselves, leading to his nervous breakdown in 1947 and a seven-month confinement at Camarillo State Hospital in California. Though he had triumphs in his final years, they were interspersed with suicide attempts, narcotics arrests and outpatient visits to the psychiatric ward of Bellevue Hospital in New York.

Parker died of a heart attack on 12 March 1955 at age 34. The coroner who performed Parker's autopsy mistakenly estimated him to be between 50 and 60 years of age.

DIZZY GILLESPIE

BEBOP ARCHITECT
LATIN JAZZ INNOVATOR

A beloved giant of jazz, John Birks "Dizzy" Gillespie was a trumpeter of unparalleled facility as well as a consummate entertainer and charismatic raconteur who brought joy to audiences all over the world. He is best remembered for his partnership with saxophonist Charlie Parker, whom he often referred to as "the other half of my heartbeat." The two revolutionized jazz in the mid 1940s with a startlingly new, rhythmically advanced sound that came to be known as bebop. In the late 1940s, Gillespie pioneered the melding of jazz and Afro-Cuban music with Cuban percussionist Chano Pozo, resulting in such groundbreaking vehicles as "Manteca" and "Cubana Be/Cubana Bop." A longstanding ambassador for jazz, he continued spreading the word into his 70s with the United Nations Orchestra, which featured an international cast of jazz musicians.

Born on 21 October 1917 in Cheraw, South Carolina, Gillespie was initially inspired by the exuberant Swing Era trumpeter Roy Eldridge. He began playing professionally at age 18 with the Frankie Fairfax Orchestra and by 1937 replaced his trumpet hero Eldridge in the Teddy Hill Orchestra, making his recording debut with the band on a version of Jelly Roll Morton's "King Porter Stomp." He joined Cab Calloway's popular band in 1939 and he remained for two years before getting fired for throwing a spitball at the exuberant bandleader during a performance (tough the real culprit was later revealed to be trumpeter Jonah Jones). Gillespie subsequently played in bands led by Ella Fitzgerald, Benny Carter, Charlie Barnet and Duke Ellington before joining the adventurous Earl Hines Orchestra in 1942 (he wrote his most famous composition, "A Night in Tunisia," while in Hines' band).

After joining Billy Eckstine's bebop big band in 1943, Gillespie found himself playing alongside such future jazz stars as Charlie Parker, Leo Parker, Art Blakey, Wardell Gray, Oscar Pettiford, Fats Navarro, Sonny Stitt and Sarah Vaughan. (Due to the American Federation of Musicians recording ban from 1942 to November 1944, that dream band was never documented). In 1944, Dizzy participated in a seminal bebop session led by tenor sax great Coleman Hawkins that introduced the Gillespie composition "Woody 'n You." By January 1945, he had teamed up with Charlie Parker to make jazz history on 52nd Street with such dazzling bebop staples as "Groovin' High," "KoKo," "Shaw Nuff," "Dizzy Atmosphere" and "Salt Peanuts," all played at unprecedented breakneck tempos. By 1946, the two virtuosos would go their separate ways but, subsequently, had a few reunions, including the legendary 1953 Massey Hall concert in Toronto which featured drummer Max Roach, pianist Bud Powell and bassist Charles Mingus

Gillespie toured with Norman Granz's Jazz at the Philharmonic revue through the 1950s. During this decade he made the first of several U.S. State Department-sponsored tours of Europe, South America and the Far East, whetting his appetite for the music of other cultures and serving as a springboard for later investigations into world music.

Gillespie led several small groups through the 1960s and in the 1970s participated in a series of recordings for the Pablo label, including encounters with fellow trumpeters Clark Terry and Roy Eldridge and pianists Oscar Peterson and Count Basie. Though his trumpet facility was diminished by the 1980s, Dizzy continued to tour and record through the decade with his United Nations Orchestra. In 1989, at age 72, he made a live duet recording in Paris with fellow bebop pioneer Max Roach. Gillespie's last two recordings — *To Bird with Love* and *To Diz with Love* — were taken from a month-long engagement at New York's Blue Note jazz club in 1992. He died a year later, on 7 January 1993, at his home in Englewood, New Jersey.

108 | Young Gillespie on 52nd Street during the late 1940s, sporting the quintessential hipster look of bop glasses, beret and goatee.

109 | Showman Dizzy posing by a bust of himself, circa 1958 during one of his U.S. State Department-sponsored tours of Europe.

110 | Gillespie in a rare introspective moment on the set of the BBC TV show "Jazz 625," circa 1964.

111 | Bebop pioneer Dizzy, seen here in 1970, also pioneered the melding of jazz and Afro-Cuban music in the late 1940s on such groundbreaking vehicles as "Manteca" and "Cubana Be/Cubana Bop."

112 | Gillespie, at age 68, strikes a reflective pose during a sound check before a performance at London's Royal Festival Hall with his United Nations Orchestra.

112-113 | Gillespie performing at the Nice Jazz Festival in 1983.

THELONIOUS MONK

THE HIGH PRIEST OF BEBOP

An idiosyncratic sculptor working with sound, Thelonious Sphere Monk carved out a place for himself in jazz history, impacting generations of jazz musicians in the process. Portrayed by some writers throughout his career as the "Mad Monk" or the "High Priest of Bop," the enigmatic pianist-composer was largely misunderstood by the masses yet praised by fellow musicians for his revolutionary approach to jazz. While mainstream scribes tended to focus on his array of wild hats and sunglasses or his eccentric onstage behavior — he often danced, wandered away from his piano and strolled the stage aimlessly or spun in place like a whirling dervish — musicians, discerning critics and astute aficionados understood the depth of Monk's profound contribution.

Melodic gems like "Ask Me Now," "Crepuscule with Nellie," "Monk's Mood," the hauntingly beautiful "Ruby, My Dear" and the gorgeous ballad "'Round Midnight" are among his numerous contributions to the standard jazz repertoire. Rhythmically tricky numbers like "Criss-Cross," "Work," "Four In One," "Epistrophy," "Evidence" and "Rhythm-a-ning" are still tackled by jazz musicians young and old. And dissonant harmonies like "Straight No Chaser," "I Mean You," "Well, You Needn't" and "Nutty" continue to resonate with startling originality. Like perfectly crafted short stories, all of these Monk tunes hold up under continual retelling and never fail to convey that "sound of surprise" that is at the heart of jazz.

Born in Rocky Mount, North Carolina in 1917, Monk moved with his family five years later to New York City and began informal piano studies at age 11. By age 16, he was playing at dances and local restaurants with a trio he had formed. After touring for two years as accompanist to a female evangelist minister and divine healer, he returned to New York and began working professionally around Harlem. In January 1941, Monk took a job as house pianist at Minton's Playhouse. The Harlem club would become a late-night hang-out for a crew of like-minded musicians, including guitarist Charlie Christian, trumpeter Dizzy Gillespie and drummer Kenny Clarke. It was at Minton's that these young modernists began experimenting with a provocative new style of jazz that came to be known as bebop. By early 1944, Monk was playing on 52nd Street in Coleman Hawkins' band. He made his first recordings as a leader, at age 30, in October 1947 for the Blue Note label. He subsequently recorded for the Prestige and Riverside labels before signing in 1962 with Columbia Records, where he made such essential recordings as *Monk's Dream*, *Criss-Cross* and *Underground* and also gained his greatest exposure, culminating in a 1964 cover story in *Time* magazine entitled "The Loneliest Monk." By the late 1960s, signs of mental illness began manifesting in Monk's alarmingly erratic public behavior. Diagnosed as having bi-polar disorder, he spent time in psychiatric hospitals, where he underwent electric shock treatment and remained on a regimen of thorazine and lithium to manage his manic-depressive state. By the early 1970s, he had sharply curtailed his public appearances, playing his last concert in 1976 at New York's Carnegie Hall. Monk lived out his life in seclusion, residing at the home of British-born jazz enthusiast, friend and patron Baroness Pannonica de Koenigswarter (namesake of Monk's delicate ballad "Pannonica") before passing away on 17 February 1982.

116 | Monk performing in France in the Spring of 1966 with his quartet of drummer Ben Riley, bassist Larry Gales and tenor saxophonist Charlie Rouse.
117 | Monk at the piano in 1940 with bebop trumpeter Howard McGhee.

ART TATUM

VIRTUOSO OF THE HIGHEST ORDER

There's a famous story that Fats Waller, upon spotting Art Tatum in the audience at one of his gigs, was reported to have said, "I just play the piano, but God is in the house tonight." A piano virtuoso of unparalleled technical ability, Tatum was a musician's musician, greatly admired by jazz and classical pianists alike. Tatum's pianistic innovations also influenced such modern jazz pianists as Bud Powell, Thelonius Monk, Oscar Peterson, Bill Evans, Herbie Hancock and Chick Corea. His protégé, the late Billy Taylor, described the exuberant, harmonically sophisticated style of his idol: "The thing that made Tatum most interesting to me was the fact that he could take a melody and extemporaneously add chords to it or play notes that he heard that complemented the melody. With his elaborate fills, his dazzling speed and sweeping runs, shifting tempos and swinging rhythms, he was a whole band, complete in himself."

Born in Toldedo, Ohio on 13 October 1909, Tatum was totally blind in one eye from infancy and almost completely blind in the other. A child prodigy with perfect pitch, he had a few years of classical training before turning to jazz, inspired first by Fats Waller and later influenced by Earl Hines. He turned pro at age 18, was hired as staff pianist at a local radio station, and the following year he began working with singer and fellow Toledo resident Jon Hendricks. Tatum came to New York for the first time in 1932, accompanying singer Adelaide Hall at a recording session. But it was his own first date as a leader in March 1933 — solo piano recordings for the Brunswick label, including a pyrotechnic rendition of "Tiger Rag" — that put Tatum on the jazz map.

With the repeal of Prohibition on 3 December 1933, he began an engagement at the Onyx Club on 52nd Street. During the early 1930s, Tatum would also engage in after-hours cutting sessions in Harlem with pianists like stride masters James P. Johnson, Willie "The Lion" Smith, Don Lambert and Fats Waller. In 1943, he formed his popular Art Tatum Trio with bassist Slam Stewart and guitarist Tiny Grimes and the following year recorded with the 1944 Esquire Jazz All-Stars, Louis Armstrong, Billie Holiday, Coleman Hawkins, Lionel Hampton and others, at the Metropolitan Opera House. In 1955, Tatum recorded a series of group sessions with Ben Webster, Jo Jones, Buddy Rich, Buddy DeFranco, Benny Carter, Harry 'Sweets' Edison and Roy Eldridge for Norman Granz's Pablo label. He died from uremia in Los Angles on 5 November 1956.

SARAH VAUGHAN THE DIVINE ONE

She possessed a magnificent voice and ranked with Ella Fitzgerald and Billie Holiday in the very top echelon of female jazz singers of the past century. With a perfectly controlled vibrato and wide expressive abilities, along with an incredible command of her instrument, Sarah Vaughan cast her spell on audiences for five decades. And while the swooping, soaring soprano of her youth had dropped in register to a sultry contralto range later in her career, she continued to carry herself with regal bearing to match her nickname, "The Divine One." And audiences openly adored her. For sheer swinging and peerless scatting technique, few could touch Sarah's frisky renditions of such bop staples as "I'll Remember April," "Sometimes I'm Happy (Sometimes I'm Blue")" and "Cherokee." But she also had the ability to melt hearts with profoundly moving interpretations of ballads like "Misty," "Lover Man," "How Long Has This Been Going On," Stephen Sondheim's "Send in the Clowns" (from *A Little Night Music*), Duke Ellington's "I Got It Bad And That Ain't Good" and Antonio Carlos Jobim's "Dindi."

Born on 27 March 1924 in Newark, New Jersey, Vaughan sang in the church choir as a child and began piano lessons at age seven. After winning a talent show at the Apollo Theater in 1942 (she impressed the judges with a remarkably mature reading of "Body and Soul"), she was hired as a singer for the Earl Hines big band in April 1943. When Billy Eckstine left the Hines band to form his own bebop big band (with such future stars as Charlie Parker, Dizzy Gillespie, Sonny Stitt, Lucky Thompson, Kenny Dorham, Gene Ammons, Leo Parker and Art Blakey), Vaughan joined him, later making her recording debut with Eckstine's outfit in 1945. After recording with John Kirby in 1946, she set out on a solo career, at first freelancing in clubs on New York's 52nd Street like the Three Deuces, the Famous Door, the Downbeat and the Onyx Club. Between 1946 and 1948, she recorded a string of hit tunes on the Musicraft label including "Tenderly," "If You Could See Me Now," "Nature Boy" and "It's Magic."

During the 1950s, Vaughan gained greater visibility through several volumes of Gershwin, Rodgers & Hart and Irving Berlin songbooks for Mercury Records along with jazz dates for the label's subsidiary, Emarcy (including a memorable 1954 recording with trumpet great Clifford Brown entitled *Sarah Vaughan*). She later recorded for Roulette (1960–1964), Mercury (1963–1967) and Mainstream (1971–1974) before hooking up with Norman Granz's Pablo label, which led to a string of superb recordings from 1977–1982 with such stellar sidemen as guitarist Joe Pass, drummer Louie Bellson, pianists Oscar Peterson and Sir Roland Hanna and bassist Ray Brown. For 1981's *Send in the Clowns*, she was accompanied by the Count Basie Orchestra.

In 1985, Vaughan received a star on the Hollywood Walk of Fame and in 1988 she was inducted into the American Jazz Hall of Fame. In 1989, the National Endowment for the Arts bestowed upon her its highest honor in jazz, the NEA Jazz Masters Award. During a run at New York's Blue Note jazz club in 1989, she received a diagnosis of lung cancer and was too ill to finish the final day of what would turn out to be her final series of public performances. She died at her home in Los Angeles on 4 April 1990 at age 66.

122 | Vaughan swinging at New York's Café Society in 1947, around the time that she scored a hit with "Tenderly." **123** | Vaughan singing "Black Coffee" into a microphone at a 1944 recording session.

124 | Vaughan backstage while singing in the Billy Eckstine Orchestra, circa 1945.

125 | Ella Fitzgerald conferring with Sarah Vaughan backstage at a Jazz at the Philharmonic show in 1957.

126 | The Divine One in the autumn of her years, acknowledging her adoring fans following her performance at the 1985 Paris Jazz Festival.

127 | For sheer swinging and peerless scatting technique, few could touch Sassy, seen here casting her spell in concert at London's Hammersmith Odeon, 1967.

"When I sing, trouble can sit right on my shoulder and I don't even notice."

Sarah Vaughan

ELLA FITZGERALD

FIRST LADY OF SONG

One of the greatest scat singers in the history of jazz, Ella Fitzgerald was a virtuoso improviser as well as a remarkable ballad interpreter. Pure tone, clear diction and an engaging, girlish, voice were the hallmarks of her straightforward singing style early on, along with her incredible three-octave range. In later years, Ella would develop her improvisational skills to such a degree that she was regarded by male musicians as "one of the cats," capable of swinging as forcefully and spontaneously as any soloist in the band.

The celebrated "First Lady of Song" was born on 25 April 1917 in Newport News, Virginia. She got her big break at age 17, winning an amateur talent show at the Apollo Theater in Harlem on 21 November 1934. Jazz saxophonist Benny Carter, who happened to be in the audience that evening, later brought Ella to the attention of drummer-bandleader Chick Webb, who hired her as the female singer for his popular orchestra, a mainstay at the Savoy Ballroom. She started out sharing vocal duties with Taft Jordan and Louis Jordan before becoming the featured singer with the band. In 1936, the Chick Webb Orchestra scored hits with Fitzgerald on "Sing Me a Swing Song" and "You'll Have to Swing It (Mr. Paganini)." But it was the catchy 1938 ditty, "A-Tisket A-Tasket," that made Ella a household name. Following Webb's death in June 1939, she took over the band, at age 22, renaming it Ella Fitzgerald and Her Famous Orchestra. She remained its leader for two years before signing as a solo artist, in late 1941, with Decca Records.

By 1945, Fitzgerald had begun to demonstrate a freer, more mature sense of phrasing while alluding to the remarkably agile Louis Armstrong-influenced scat prowess that would become her trademark. Beginning in 1948, the year she married the great jazz bassist Ray Brown, Ella became a favorite on Norman Granz's Jazz at the Philharmonic concert tours, unleashing her formidable scatting chops in the company of such jazz stars as Dizzy Gillespie, Flip Phillips, Roy Eldridge, Herb Ellis and Oscar Peterson. During this period, she scored a hit with her scat-laden version of "Lady Be Good," which would become her trademark throughout the rest of her career. Fitzgerald's profile rose in the 1950s through a series of popular Songbook recordings, for Verve, dedicated to the works of Duke Ellington, Cole Porter, Jerome Kern, Irving Berlin, Johnny Mercer, Harold Arlen and George and Ira Gershwin. One of the most rewarding albums of that series was her 1958 encounter with Louis Armstrong on Gershwin's *Porgy & Bess*.

In 1960, she scored another hit with her swinging, upbeat reading of Kurt Weill's "Mack the Knife." After bouncing between several different labels through the decade, she emerged in the 1970s on Norman Granz's Pablo label with a series of classy small-group recordings featuring Joe Pass, Oscar Peterson and Count Basie. Ella fell into ill health in the 1980s, was admitted to intensive care for heart trouble in 1986, then made a comeback in 1990, performing in a London concert with the Count Basie Orchestra. By 1994, she was in retirement, confined to a wheelchair. She died two years later on 14 June 1996.

"Just don't give up trying to do what you really want to do. Where there is love and inspiration, I don't think you can go wrong."

Ella Fitzgerald

130 | Ella Fitzgerald relaxing at the piano with her husband, bassist Ray Brown, in a 1947 photo.

131 | Ella Fitzgerald in the studio, circa 1948-1949, during the time she recorded her live *Royal Roost Sessions* on 52nd Street with the Ray Brown Trio & Quintet.

132 | Ella Fitzgerald conferring with movie star Marilyn Monroe at the Tiffany Club in Hollywood, 1954, the year she recorded *Songs in a Mellow Mood* for Decca.

132-133 | Ella on the set of the 1955 film *Pete Kelly's Blues*, with director-actor Jack Webb, discussing the finer points of the script and her cameo appearance as singer Maggie Jackson.

BUDDY RICH

'THE WORLD'S GREATEST DRUMMER'

Once regarded as "The World's Greatest Drummer," Buddy Rich's career spanned seven decades – from his appearances on the vaudeville circuit as a child star to collaborations in the 1940s and the 1950s with jazz legends like Charlie Parker, Dizzy Gillespie, Art Tatum, Lester Young and Coleman Hawkins to his own legendary tenure as a big band leader through the 1960s, the 1970s and into the 1980s. Rich's uncanny speed and precision on the drum kit, along with his phenomenal endurance, marked him as one of the great instrumental virtuosos of the 20th century. An irascible figure and a demanding bandleader, Rich was known, both on and off stage, for his tough persona and caustic wit. But, he is remembered as a champion of the drums and one of jazz's larger-than-life figures. According to Gene Krupa, a jazz drumming legend from a previous generation, Rich was "The greatest drummer ever to have drawn breath."

Born in Brooklyn on 30 September 1917, Rich's parents were vaudevillians who recognized his uncanny ability, at age one, to keep a steady beat with spoons. Buddy actually began playing drums when he was 18 months old and as a four-year-old was billed on the vaudeville circuit as "Traps the Drum Wonder." At the peak of Rich's childhood career, he was reportedly the second-highest paid child entertainer in the world (after Jackie Coogan, who played opposite Charlie Chaplin in the 1921 silent film, *The Kid*). At age 11, young Buddy was performing as a bandleader, though he had received no formal drum instruction. His earliest jazz drumming influences included Chick Webb, Gene Krupa, Dave Tough and Count Basie's drummer "Papa" Jo Jones.

Rich broke into the jazz scene in 1937 with Joe Marsala's group and, subsequently, worked with such prominent players as trumpeter Bunny Berigan (1938) and clarinetist and big band leader Artie Shaw (1939). From 1939 to 1945 he worked in Tommy Dorsey's big band where he met the up-and-coming singer Frank Sinatra. Rich played frequently on Norman Granz's Jazz at the Philharmonic concerts during the 1950s, driving small groups that included the likes of Art Tatum, Ella Fitzgerald, Charlie Parker, Lionel Hampton and Lester Young. He also worked in big bands led by Harry James, Les Brown and Charlie Ventura before forming his own 17-piece orchestra in 1966. He is most famous for his innovative adaptations of Leonard Bernstein's "West Side Story Medley," the Beatles' "Norwegian Wood," Chick Corea's "La Fiesta" and Bill Reddie's "Channel One Suite."

Rich continued to lead a swinging big band until his death, at age 69, on 2 April 1987 following surgery for a malignant brain tumor. Longtime friend, Frank Sinatra, delivered a touching eulogy at Rich's funeral. Since Rich's death, a number of memorial concerts have been held. In 1994, the Rich tribute album *Burning for Buddy: A Tribute to the Music of Buddy Rich* was released. Produced by Rush drummer/lyricist Neil Peart, it features performances of Rich staples by such renowned drummers such as Kenny Aronoff, Dave Weckl, Steve Gadd, Max Roach, Steve Smith and Peart himself, accompanied by the Buddy Rich Big Band. Former Journey drummer Smith released his own 1999 tribute album, *Buddy's Buddies*, and followed it in 2003 with Buddy's Buddies' *Very Live at Ronnie Scott's London*.

MAX ROACH

BEBOP PIONEER
MUSICAL DRUMMER

Widely considered one of the most important drummers in jazz history, Max Roach worked with such il-lustrious figures as Coleman Hawkins, Dizzy Gillespie, Charlie Parker, Miles Davis, Duke Ellington, Charles Mingus, Sonny Rollins and Clifford Brown. He also led his own innovative groups through the 1960s and made numerous musical statements relating to the civil rights movement of African Ameri-cans.

One of the architects of bebop (along with Charlie Parker, Dizzy Gillespie and fellow drummer Kenny Clarke), Roach was born on 10 January 1924 in Newland, North Carolina and began playing drums in a gospel band at age 10. After studying at the Manhattan School of Music, he became the house drum-mer at Minton's Playhouse in Harlem, where he encountered cutting edge players of the day like Park-er, Gillespie and Thelonious Monk. He had brief stints in bands led by Benny Carter and Duke Ellington before joining Dizzy Gillespie's quintet in 1943. Roach made his recording debut that year with Coleman Hawkins.

By 1945, Roach was playing on 52nd Street in Charlie Parker's band. His revolutionary approach to the kit, which shifted the rhythmic focus from the bass drum to the ride cymbal, freed up drummers and fu-eled the early bebop movement. Roach later recorded with trumpet greats Miles Davis and Kenny Dorham and also participated in the historic *Birth of the Cool* sessions in 1948 with Davis, Lee Konitz, J.J. Johnson, John Lewis, Gerry Mulligan, Gunther Schuller and others. In the early 1950s, he toured with the Jazz at the Philharmonic revue before forming his own groundbreaking hard bop quintet with the influential young trumpet star Clifford Brown in 1954. They recorded three superb albums together, including the live 1956 album *At Basin Street*, before Brown was tragically killed in a car accident with the band's pianist, Richie Powell, in June 1956.

In 1960, at the outset of the burgeoning civil rights movement, Roach created the politically-charged five-part *We Insist!: Freedom Now Suite*. This crusading protest work featured his activist wife, singer Abbey Lincoln (to whom he was married from 1962 until 1970), along with trombonist Julian Priester, trumpeter Booker Little, the legendary tenor saxophonist Coleman Hawkins and percussionists Ray Mantilla and Michael Olatunji.

Roach followed up with the classic 1961 landmark *Percussion Bitter Sweet*, which featured such stellar sidemen as trumpeter Booker Little, alto saxophonist Eric Dolphy, trombonist Julian Priester, tenor

139 | The innovative drummer and bebop pioneer Max Roach, who played with Charlie Parker, Miles Davis, Thelonious Monk, Bud Powell, Sonny Rollins and Clifford Brown, strikes a pose in 1990.

saxophonist Clifford Jordan, pianist Mal Waldron, bassist Art Davis and singer Abbey Lincoln, who contributed emotionally stirring vocals on "Mendacity." Roach's 1965 classic *Drums Unlimited* included three unaccompanied drumming showcases in "For Big Sid," "The Drum Also Waltzes" and the dramatic title track. In 1970, he formed the innovative 7-piece ensemble M'Boom, which explored the melodic possibilities of drums and percussion.

During the 1970s, Roach recorded riveting duets with saxophonist Anthony Braxton and pianist Cecil Taylor. He continued to perform through the 1980s with M'Boom, his working quartet and his Double Quartet (featuring the Uptown String Quartet, which included his daughter Maxine Roach on viola). Roach remained an adventurous spirit in his later years, performing with orchestras, dance companies, Japanese folklore musicians and even rappers and break dancers. He had a triumphant reunion with his bebop colleague Dizzy Gillespie on *Max & Dizzy: Paris 1989*. Roach's last recording, 2002's *Friendship*, was an encounter with trumpeter Clark Terry. He died on 15 August 2007 after a long illness.

140 | Max Roach in concert in 1965, the year he recorded his classic *Drums Unlimited* album, which features several tracks of melodic, brilliantly constructed drum solos.

141 | Max Roach on the kit at Rudy Van Gelder's Studio in Hackensack, New Jersey, during a session for tenor saxophonist Johnny Griffin's 1956 Blue Note debut.

142-143 | Max Roach and his longtime friend and colleague, trumpeter Dizzy Gillespie, in a Paris studio during the recording session for their 1989 duet album. **143 |** Fellow Brooklynites and former schoolmates Randy Weston and Max Roach, performing a duet concert in 1997.

"Jazz is a very democratic musical form. It comes out of a communal experience. We take our respective instruments and collectively create a thing of beauty."

Max Roach

MILES DAVIS

THE PICASSO OF JAZZ

Considered one of the most important musicians of the 20th century, Miles Davis's impact on jazz cannot be overstated. Several of his compositions have become part of the jazz canon. He also recorded the best-selling album in jazz history, 1959's *Kind of Blue*, which has sold four million copies to date. Gil Evans called him "a great singer of songs" for his uncanny lyricism and remarkably expressive quality on trumpet while Duke Ellington likened him to Picasso for the many different musical styles he traversed in his celebrated career. Davis' restlessly creative nature kept him constantly moving forward, and he pursued each new avenue with conviction. As Evans put it, "A lot of other musicians are constantly looking around to hear what the next person is doing and they worry about whether they themselves are in style. Miles has confidence in his own taste, and he goes his own way."

Born on 26 May 1926 in Alton, Illinois, Davis had a comfortable upper-middle-class upbringing in East St. Louis. He began playing trumpet in school, drawing inspiration from Clark Terry. After apprenticing at age 17 with Eddie Randle's Blue Devils, he sat in with the Billy Eckstine Orchestra when it came to his hometown in July, 1944. Playing alongside Dizzy Gillespie and Charlie Parker in Eckstine's band prompted his move to New York by September. While studying classical music by day at Juilliard, Davis would seek out Charlie Parker and the beboppers each night on 52nd Street. He soon dropped out of Juilliard and by November, 1945 had appeared on Bird's first record as a leader for Savoy, soloing on "Now's the Time."

In 1948, Davis organized a nonet to rehearse new compositions arranged by Gil Evans, Gerry Mulligan and John Lewis. Their historic *Birth of the Cool* sessions in early 1949 marked the first of many triumphs for Davis. In 1957, he led a string of superb hard bop sessions for Prestige (*Cookin'*, *Workin'*, *Relaxin'*, *Steamin'*) with his quintet of saxophonist John Coltrane, pianist Red Garland, bassist Paul Chambers and drummer Philly Joe Jones. In the late 1950s and early 1960s, for Columbia, he recorded the modal classics *Milestones* and *Kind of Blue* as well as three orchestral collaborations with Evans — *Miles Ahead*, *Porgy & Bess* and *Sketches of Spain*.

In the mid 1960s, with his quintet of saxophonist Wayne Shorter, pianist Herbie Hancock, bassist Ron Carter and drummer Tony Williams, Davis released a string of recordings that ranks among the greatest of the period, including *E.S.P.*, *Miles Smiles*, *Sorcerer* and *Nefertiti*. His gradual transition to jazz-rock began in 1968 with *Filles de Kilimanjaro* (his first recording to employ electric piano), continued with 1969's *In A Silent Way* (with electric guitarist John McLaughlin and electric keyboardists Joe Zawinul and Chick Corea) and culminated with 1970's *Bitches Brew*, his full-blown fusion manifesto. Davis' electric phase continued through the 1970s with *A Tribute to Jack Johnson*, *Live-Evil*, *On The Corner*, *Big Fun* and *Get Up With It*. Following his turbulent live releases, *Agharta* and *Pangaea*, recorded in Japan in 1975,

146 | Miles Davis sits with his trumpet in a reflective moment in the studio in 1959, around the time of recording session for his historic *Kind of Blue*.

147 | By 1969, Miles' music was changing, as was his fashion sense. Through the influence of second wife, Betty Mabry, he switched from wearing suits to a more flowing, looser clothing style.

148 and 149 | In 1987, the "Prince of Darkness" was touring on the strength of two acclaimed Warner Bros. albums produced by bassist Marcus Miller, *Tutu* and *Amandla*.

150 | Miles Davis strikes a classic pose, trumpet pointed downward, in a Chicago concert with his celebrated 'comeback band' of 1982.

151 | The enigmatic Miles Davis wearing wrap-around shades and an audacious blue suit, playing his signature red trumpet and Harmon mute in a 1986 concert.

Davis went into retirement. He re-emerged in 1980 with a string of potent recordings through the decade, including *The Man With The Horn*, *We Want Miles*, *Decoy* and *You're Under Arrest* for Columbia and two acclaimed Marcus Miller-produced projects for Warner Bros., *Tutu* and *Amandla*.

On 8 July 1991, Davis shocked the jazz world by joining an orchestra conducted by Quincy Jones at the Montreux Jazz Festival to perform his old *Sketches of Spain/Miles Ahead/Porgy & Bess* material. It marked the first time in his long and celebrated career that Miles ever looked back. He died shortly after that gala concert, on 28 September 1991. His last recording, a collaboration with rapper Easy Mo Bee titled *Doo-Bop*, was released posthumously in 1992.

152-153 | Miles Davis at the North Sea Jazz Festival in Den Haag on 14 July 1991, just two months before he died.

154 | Miles Davis in typically colorful garb, performing at the Vienna Jazz Festival on 12 July 1991 with Kenny Garrett, Deron Johnson, Ricky Wellman, Foley and Richard Patterson.

155 | Duke Ellington likened the restlessly creative Miles Davis to Picasso for the many different musical styles he traversed in his celebrated career.

BUD POWELL

THE CHARLIE PARKER OF PIANO

A beacon of bebop, Bud Powell successfully transferred the dazzling speed and dexterity of Charlie Parker's alto sax flights to the piano. His early recordings for the Roost, Verve and Blue Note labels between 1947 and 1951 represent the apex of jazz piano playing, ranking right alongside the great Art Tatum. However, his career was hampered by psychiatric problems. A tormented soul through the 1940s and 1950s, Powell endured lengthy stays in mental institutions, where he underwent electroshock therapy. He died on 31 July 1966 of tuberculosis, malnutrition and alcoholism.

Born in Harlem on 27 September 1924, Earl Rudolph "Bud" Powell took up piano at age six. Inspired by Tatum and Fats Waller, he dropped out of school at age 15 and began playing around Harlem and Greenwich Village. After his gigs, he would head to Minton's Playhouse in Harlem, where his friend and mentor Thelonious Monk introduced him to players experimenting with a new music that would later be known as bebop. In 1944, Powell joined the Cootie Williams Orchestra and later that year played on the band's rendition of Monk's "'Round Midnight." In 1945, he was savagely beaten by the police, which may have exacerbated a pre-existing mental condition.

Powell recorded his first session as a leader in 1947. He played on a Charlie Parker session with Miles Davis, Tommy Potter and Max Roach in May of that year and in November he was admitted to Creedmoor Psychiatric Center, where he remained for a year and first encountered electroshock therapy. Powell returned to the public arena in 1949 with his first Blue Note recording, *The Amazing Bud Powell*, which featured Fats Navarro, Sonny Rollins, Tommy Potter and Roy Haynes and introduced his famous compositions "Dance of the Infidels" and "Bouncing with Bud." Powell's follow-up on Blue Note, a 1951 trio session with Curly Russell and Max Roach, introduced his classic compositions "Parisian Thoroughfare" and "Un Poco Loco." There followed another long stay in a mental hospital, from late 1951 to early 1953. Upon his release, and while taking medication to combat schizophrenia, Powell recorded again for Blue Note. But he suffered another emotional setback in June 1956 when his pianist brother Richie Powell and trumpeter Clifford Brown were killed in a car crash.

In 1959, Powell took up residency in Paris, where he remained for four years and recorded with fellow expatriates like Dexter Gordon, Johnny Griffin and Kenny Clarke. But Powell's playing on these recordings never approached the heights of his former glory days. Upon returning to New York, in 1964, he recorded his final album, *The Return of Bud Powell*, less than two years before his death.

157 | Young John Earl Powell stands behind his father Bud Powell during a session in December, 1958 for his Blue Note album, *The Scene Changes*.

BILL EVANS

NEW IMPRESSIONS
FOR PIANO

One of the most influential pianists over the last 50 years, Bill Evans pioneered a new direction in jazz that emphasized harmonic extrapolation and an exquisite, walking-on-eggshells sensitivity more than the macho, two-fisted, blues-based swing-style of the previous generation of players. Evans' crystalline, Erik Satie-inspired approach to the keyboard would have a huge impact on the generations of players who followed in his wake, including Chick Corea, Keith Jarrett, Denny Zeitlin, Steve Kuhn, Marc Copland, Richie Beirach, Fred Hersch, Michel Petrucciani, Bill Charlap and Brad Mehldau.

A former member of the Miles Davis sextet, Evans made a lasting impression with his first trio featuring the innovative bassist Scott LaFaro and sensitive drummer Paul Motian. Their 1961 live album *Sunday at the Village Vanguard* set the standard for interactive trio work and is still regarded as a jazz classic.

Born on 16 August 1929 in Plainfield, New Jersey, Evans began piano lessons at age six. After graduating as a piano major from Southeastern Louisiana University in 1950, he toured briefly with Herbie Fields' band before being drafted into the Army. After three years of service, Evans moved to New York, in 1954, and began playing in clarinetist Tony Scott's quartet while pursuing postgraduate studies at Mannes College, where he met and began collaborating with composer-theoretician George Russell. By 1956, Evans had recorded his first album as a leader, *New Jazz Conceptions*, which included the first incarnation of one of his best-known compositions, the delicate "Waltz for Debby."

During his eight-month tenure with the Miles Davis Sextet, Evans put his zen-like stamp on the landmark 1959 recording *Kind of Blue*, the biggest-selling acoustic jazz album of all time. The album's strikingly atmospheric pieces "Blue in Green" and "Flamenco Sketches," both co-composed by Evans, reveal his delicate touch and a European harmonic sensibility inspired by such French impressionists as Debussy and Ravel. After leaving Davis' sextet, Evans combined forces in December of 1958 with the astounding young bassist Scott LaFaro and drummer Paul Motian in a near-telepathic trio. Following such successful Riverside albums as 1958's meditative *Everybody Digs Bill Evans*, 1959's *Portrait in Jazz* and especially 1961's *Sunday at the Village Vanguard*, Evans became a bona fide jazz star. Just ten days after recording that Vanguard landmark in June 1961, LaFaro was killed in an auto accident at age 25.

Shattered by the tragedy, Evans went into seclusion for a year, returning to the scene in 1962 with *Undercurrent*, the first of two meetings on record in a duo format with guitarist and kindred spirit Jim Hall.

159 | Influential pianist Bill Evans at the 1967 Newport Jazz Festival, appearing with bassist Eddie Gomez and drummer Philly Joe Jones.

Evans followed with recordings in a variety of settings, including sessions with Gary McFarland's big band, saxophonist and label mate Stan Getz, singer Tony Bennett and a full orchestra with arrangements by Claus Ogerman. He even experimented with overdubbing on the controversial *Conversations With Myself*. In 1968, Evans formed his second definitive trio with bassist Eddie Gomez and drummer Marty Morell. They remained together for seven years and recorded some of Evans' most famous pieces, including "Re: Person I Knew," "T.T.T. (Twelve Tone Tune)," "Since We Met" and "Sugar Plum." By early 1975, Morell had left the trio and was replaced by Eliot Zigmund. Evans' last trio, with bassist Marc Johnson and drummer Joe La Barbera, remained together from 1978 until early 1980. Plagued by a heroin and cocaine addiction throughout his career, the great pianist-composer died on 15 September 1980 at age 51 from a hemorrhaging ulcer and bronchial pneumonia.

160-161 | Composer Bill Evans going over a musical score at the Jazzhouse in Copenhagen, Denmark, 1964.

162-163 | Bill Evans in concert at the Keystone Korner in San Francisco, August 1980, shortly before his death on 15 September.

"Bill was both a great creative
artist and a virtuoso pianist,
and in addition, I heard from
him some of the greatest
accompaniment I know of in
music. He added an immeasur-
able contribution to American
music. He was my friend and
I miss him."

Chick Corea

SONNY ROLLINS

SAXOPHONE COLOSSUS

Tenor titan Sonny Rollins is perhaps the greatest living saxophonist. A revered figure in jazz with a long and rich history involving tenures with Miles Davis, Bud Powell, Clifford Brown and Thelonious Monk, Rollins is a perennial poll-winner who continues to blow with ferocious power and uncommon authority into his 80s. A product of the bebop and hard bop eras who was heavily influenced by both Charlie Parker and Lester Young, Rollins is a melodic improviser of the highest order with a stunning harmonic imagination. In concert or on record, he never fails to deliver the sound of surprise.

Born Theodore Walter Rollins in New York City on 7 September 1930, he started playing the piano at age nine and took up the alto saxophone at age 16, inspired by Louis Jordan. Falling under the spell of Coleman Hawkins, he switched to tenor sax after graduating from high school. Rollins first recorded in 1948 with bebop vocalist Babs Gonzales. There followed sessions in 1949 with Bud Powell and Fats Navarro and, in 1951, with Miles Davis. He made a string of superb recordings as a sideman with Thelonious Monk, culminating with 1957s *Brilliant Corners*. In 1956, he played on the seminal hard bop album, *Clifford Brown & Max Roach at Basin Street*. Rollins also made many landmark recordings as a leader during the 1950s, including *Saxophone Colossus* and *Tenor Madness* (with John Coltrane) in 1956, *Way Out West* (with Shelly Manne and Ray Brown) and *A Night at the Village Vanguard* (with Elvin Jones) in 1957 and *Freedom Suite* (with Max Roach) in 1958.

But between 1959 and 1961, Rollins left the music business to pursue a spiritual path, visiting Japan and India and studying yoga and Zen. He returned in 1962, recording his groundbreaking comeback album *The Bridge* with guitarist Jim Hall. The following year, he recorded with one of his tenor idols, Coleman Hawkins, on *Sonny Meets Hawk!*, which also featured trumpeter Don Cherry.

Rollins continued recording prolifically through the 1960s and 1970s for the RCA/Victor, Impulse and Milestone labels, and in 1978 toured as a member of the Milestone Jazzstars (with McCoy Tyner, Ron Carter and Al Foster). In 1981, he appeared as a special guest soloist on the Rolling Stone's *Tattoo You* and continued with a string of acclaimed recordings as a leader through the 1980s (*G-Man*, *Reel Life*, *Sunny Days Starry Nights* and *Dancing in the Dark*) and 1990s (*Here's to the People*, *Old Flames*, *Plus Three* and *Global Warming*). Rollins won his first Grammy Award for 2000's *This Is What I Do*.

On 11 September 2001, the 71-year-old Rollins, who lived just blocks away from the World Trade Center, was forced to evacuate his apartment with saxophone in hand when the Twin Towers collapsed. Five days later he played a concert at the Berklee School of Music in Boston. A live recording of that performance was released in 2005 as *Without a Song: The 9/11 Concert*, earning Rollins his second Grammy Award. In 2006, Rollins formed his own label, Doxy (named after one of his tunes), and released the CD *Sonny, Please*. He celebrated his 80th birthday in September 2010 with a gala performance at New York's Beacon Theater with guest appearances by Ornette Coleman, Jim Hall and Roy Haynes.

"I guess fortunate that I'm still around and I emphasize I guess because you never can tell what musicians would be playing had they been around as long as I have."

Sonny Rollins

JOHN COLTRANE
GIANT STEPS TO THE NEW THING

Emerging from important sideman work with Miles Davis and Thelonious Monk in the 1950s, tenor saxophonist John Coltrane would become one of the most powerfully galvanizing forces in the history of jazz. An intellectual and intensely passionate player, he came to redefine the way the tenor saxophone was played through the course of his astonishingly productive but brief career as a leader during the 1960s.

Born on 23 September 1926 in Hamlet, North Carolina, Coltrane's remarkable musical journey began in Philadelphia, where he played in R&B joints and walked the bar with his tenor sax. Following a stint in the Navy from 1945-1946, he played in the King Kolax band and in Jimmy Heath's big band through 1947. Following a tour of one-nighters with Eddie "Cleanhead" Vinson in 1948, he joined Dizzy Gillespie's big band in 1949 as lead alto player, later appearing on Gillespie's 1951 small group recording for Savoy, *School Days*. He gained further seasoning by touring with Earl Bostic in 1952 and playing in Johnny Hodges' nonet in late 1953 (he is billed as "Johnny Coltrane" on Hodges' 1954 Verve release, *Used to Be Duke*). By September, 1955, he had been hired to replace Sonny Rollins in the Miles Davis quintet featuring pianist Red Garland, bassist Paul Chambers and drummerr Philly Joe Jones. That formidable lineup set a new standard of excellence on a series of recordings for Prestige during the mid 1950s — *Cookin'*, *Relaxin'*, *Workin'* and *Steamin'* — as well as on 1956's *'Round About Midnight* on Columbia. Coltrane would leave Davis' group in April, 1957 under particularly strained circumstances. (The saxophonist had a heroin addiction during his tenure with Miles, who ultimately fired him for his unreliable attendance at gigs.)

By the summer of 1957, Coltrane had had a spiritual awakening, had kicked his heroin habit and had entered into a period of intensive woodshedding. By July of that year he had begun an extended engagement at the Five Spot Café in Thelonious Monk's quartet featuring Wilbur Ware (and later Ahmed Abdul-Malik) on bass and Shadow Wilson (alternating with Roy Haynes) on drums. It was in that setting, playing Monk's challenging music on a nightly basis, that Coltrane began developing his startling "sheets of sound" approach that would become his signature. Coltrane's work with Monk that summer sent shockwaves through the jazz community. As trombonist J.J. Johnson said to critic Ira Gitler: "Since Charlie Parker, the most electrifying sound I've heard in contemporary jazz was Coltrane playing with Monk at the Five Spot. It was incredible, like Diz and Bird."

173 | John Coltrane in a 1965 publicity photo for Impulse! Records. Ironically, he's holding a flute, which he recorded with only once, on "Syeeda's Song Flute" from 1959's *Giant Steps*.

1957 was a banner year for Coltrane. Aside from his summer residency at the Five Spot with Monk and their historic Carnegie Hall performance in November, he also released his own debut as a leader (*Coltrane* on Prestige) and recorded the classic *Blue Train* for the Blue Note label, while also appearing on sessions led by Red Garland, Mal Waldron, Art Taylor, Kenny Burrell and others. By 1958, Coltrane had rejoined Miles Davis' band and recorded such landmarks as 1958's *Milestones* and the 1959 modal masterpiece *Kind of Blue* (the best-selling jazz album of all time). That same pivotal year, he debuted on Atlantic with the harmonically complicated *Giant Steps* (the title track remains a proving ground for jazz musicians to this day) and the following year introduced the soprano sax (an instrument previously associated with Sidney Bechet) on *My Favorite Things*, the first recording to document the classic Coltrane quartet of pianist McCoy Tyner, bassist Jimmy Garrison and drummer Elvin Jones.

For Impulse!, the fledgling label which advertised itself as "The New Wave in Jazz," Coltrane recorded 1962's exquisite *Ballads*, the super-charged *Live at the Village Vanguard*, 1964's *Crescent* and his immortal work *A Love Supreme*, along with 1965's envelope-pushing offerings like *Transition* and *First Meditations*. He introduced an expanded ensemble on the free jazz manifesto *Ascension*, which featured tenor players Archie Shepp and Pharoah Sanders and trumpeter Freddie Hubbard. He introduced a second drummer, Rashied Ali, on the intensely probing *Meditations*. Coltrane's wife, pianist Alice McLeod, replaced Tyner in the lineup in 1966, appearing on *Live at the Village Vanguard Again!* Coltrane's last recording in February, 1967 — a series of provocative duets with drummer Rashied Ali — was released posthumously as *Interstellar Space*. His final performance was in Baltimore on 7 May 1967. He died of liver cancer on 17 July 1967, two months before his 41st birthday.

ART
BLAKEY

A powerful drummer of volcanic intensity, Art Blakey was the rhythmic dynamo behind his Jazz Messengers for four decades. In the tradition of drummer-bandleader and mentor Chick Webb before him, Blakey orchestrated from the kit, lighting fires on the bandstand beneath his potent soloists. "There are times when Art is so much on fire that he almost drives you off the bandstand," said trumpet great Freddie Hubbard of the hard bop pioneer. "After you play with him it feels empty playing with most other drummers."

A charismatic and larger-than-life presence on the bandstand, Blakey also had keen instincts as a talent scout. Throughout the long life of the Jazz Messengers (1954–1990), the list of players who passed through the ranks reads like a Who's Who of Jazz. During the 1950s, the Jazz Messengers, at one time or another, included trumpeters Donald Byrd, Clifford Brown, Kenny Dorham and Lee Morgan; saxophonists Hank Mobley and Benny Golson; pianists Sam Dockery and Bobby Timmons; and bassists Spanky Debrest and Jymie Merritt. In the 1960s the Jazz Messengers lineup, expanded to a sextet for classic albums like *Free For All*, *Indestructible*, *Caravan* and *Buhaina's Delight*, featured trumpeter Freddie Hubbard, tenor saxophonist Wayne Shorter, trombonist Curtis Fuller, pianist Cedar Walton and bassist Reggie Workman. Later lineups included the likes of trumpeters Woody Shaw, Randy Brecker, Chuck Mangione, Wynton Marsalis and Terence Blanchard; saxophonists Billy Harper, Bobby Watson, Branford Marsalis, Donald Harrison and Kenny Garrett; pianists John Hicks, Ronnie Mathews, James Williams, Mulgrew Miller and Benny Green; trombonists Robin Eubanks, Frank Lacy and Steve Davis; and bassists Cameron Brown, Charles Fambrough and Peter Washington. During its heyday, Blakey's Jazz Messengers introduced such jazz anthems as Bobby Timmons' "Moanin'," Benny Golson's "Blues March" and Wayne Shorter's "Lester Left Town."

A stalwart on New York's 52nd Street scene during the height of bebop in the mid-1940s, Blakey set the pace for such musical innovators as Charlie Parker, Clifford Brown, Miles Davis, Bud Powell and Thelonious Monk. During his reign with the Jazz Messengers he became an international ambassador for jazz.

Born in Pittsburgh, on 11 October 1919, Blakey was a self-taught pianist who led a big band by age 15. He switched to drums after being displaced on piano, in his own band, by fellow Pittsburgh native Erroll Garner. His biggest drumming influences as a teenager were Chick Webb and Big Sid Catlett,

both of whom would later become important mentors for him. In 1942, Blakey traveled to New York as a member of pianist Mary Lou Williams' band and the following year he toured with Fletcher Henderson's big band. In 1944, he joined Billy Eckstine's bebop big band, which included such emerging young lions as Charlie Parker, Dizzy Gillespie, Sonny Stitt, Dexter Gordon and Leo Parker. Unfortunately, that band was never documented due to a prevailing record strike imposed by the president of the American Federation of Musicians.

Following an eye-opening trip to West Africa in 1949, Blakey converted to Islam and took the Muslim name Abdullah Ibn Buhaina. That year he formed a group called the 17 Messengers, which included such stellar players as trumpeter Kenny Dorham, saxophonist Sonny Rollins, pianist Bud Powell and alto saxophonist Sahib Shihab. By 1954, Blakey and pianist Horace Silver were co-leading the first quintet edition of the Jazz Messengers, which included tenor saxophonist Hank Mobley, trumpeter Kenny Dorham and bassist Doug Watkins. When the other charter members left in 1956, Blakey carried on the band name and continued to wave the flag for hard bop as leader of the Jazz Messengers through the 1960s, the 1970s and the 1980s. His final recording, *One For All*, was made in April 1990. The much loved bandleader and jazz elder died later that year, on 16 October, just five days after his 71st birthday.

HORACE SILVER

FATHER OF FUNKY HARD BOP

An early practitioner of hard bop, pianist-composer Horace Silver has had a profound impact on Mainstream Jazz with his distinctively funky style of playing and his catchy, enduring tunes like "Sister Sadie," "Filthy McNasty," "Opus de Funk," "The Preacher," "Señor Blues" and "Serenade to a Soul Sister," all of which have become part of the jazz canon. An exponent of what he called "meaningful simplicity" on the piano, Silver began working in a trio setting during the early 1950s, led a potent quintet through the 1960s and continued touring and composing prolifically into the 1990s. An original member of the Jazz Messengers, the group he briefly co-led with Art Blakey, Silver has performed and recorded in small group and big band settings over the years. As a pianist, his blues and gospel-tinged style has influenced generations of players from Bobby Timmons, Ramsey Lewis and Les McCann through Chick Corea, Herbie Hancock and Cecil Taylor to Cyrus Chestnut, John Medeski and Bill Charlap.

Born on 2 September 1928 in Norwalk, Connecticut, his Portuguese-speaking father John Tavares Silva had emigrated to the United States from the Cape Verde Islands. (Silver paid tribute to his roots on the classic 1965 Blue Note album, *Cape Verdean Blues*). Originally a tenor saxophonist, he switched to piano in high school and became profoundly influenced by such great players as Art Tatum, Bud Powell, Teddy Wilson, Thelonious Monk and Nat "King" Cole. In 1950, at age 22, he was discovered by saxophonist Stan Getz, who hired Silver's working trio as a backing band for his own concert in Hartford. Silver worked with Getz for a year before moving to New York in 1951 and freelancing around the city with such established jazz artists as Coleman Hawkins, Lester Young and Oscar Pettiford. He played his first Blue Note session (a date led by alto saxophonist Lou Donaldson) in 1952 and, later that year, had his own debut as a leader on the renowned jazz label. In 1954, the year he was named *Down Beat* magazine's New Star, Silver joined forces with Art Blakey to co-lead The Jazz Messengers. They recorded a few albums together for Blue Note but in 1956 Silver left the band to record on his own. His prolific output as a leader for Blue Note through the 1950s and 1960s (including his 1964 hit single, "Song for My Father") established Silver as a major force in jazz.

His bands through the 1970s included such future stars as drummer Billy Cobham, tenor saxophonists Michael Brecker and Bob Berg and trumpeters Randy Brecker and Tom Harrell. He formed his own private Silveto label in the 1980s and returned to major label status with 1993's *It's Got to be Funky* on Columbia. His last recording as a leader (for the GRP label) was 1999's *Jazz Has a Sense of Humor*, a credo that the self-proclaimed "Hard Bop Grandpop" carried throughout his illustrious career. Silver told his colorful life story in his 2006 autobiography, *Let's Get To The Nitty Gritty*.

182 | Young Horace Silver at the piano in the studio during a session with the Jazz Messengers on 15 April 1956. **182-183** | Horace Silver's catchy, enduring tunes like "Sister Sadie," "Filthy McNasty," "Opus de Funk," "The Preacher," "Señor Blues" and "Serenade to a Soul Sister" have become part of the jazz canon.

STAN GETZ

THE SOUND
THE SWING
THE SAMBA

At the peak of his powers, Stan Getz had other tenor sax players standing in awe of his impeccable technique, flawless intonation and robust sound on the instrument. Even John Coltrane is reputed to have said of Getz, "We'd all sound like that if we could." One influential jazz critic during the 1950s was so enamored with Getz's golden tenor tone that he dubbed it The Sound, and the phrase stuck throughout the saxophonist's illustrious career.

A beautiful ballad interpreter as well as an inveterate swinger, Getz emulated the cool style of tenor saxophonist Lester Young. Acknowledged as a ferocious improviser who could stand toe-to-toe with beboppers like Dizzy Gillespie, Miles Davis and Sonny Stitt during the 1950s, Getz also pioneered the marriage of Brazilian music to jazz with a string of important recordings during the 1960s. The success of his *Jazz Samba*, an influential album he recorded in 1962 with guitarist Charlie Byrd, helped trigger the bossa nova craze that swept the United States in the pre-Beatles 1960s. He followed that success with a string of bossa nova albums, including *Big Band Bossa Nova* with Gary McFarland and *Jazz Samba Encore* with Brazilian guitarist-composer Luiz Bonfa. But it was 1963's *Getz/Gilberto*, his collaboration with Joao Gilberto, Antonio Carlos Jobim and Brazilian vocalist Astrud Gilberto (who had sung the alluring hit single "The Girl From Ipanema") that made Getz a household name.

Born Stanley Gayetsky on 2 February 1927 in Philadelphia, Pennsylvania, he grew up in New York City and began playing saxophone at age 13. By age 16, he had served an invaluable apprenticeship with Jack Teagarden's big band before playing in groups led by Stan Kenton (1944–1945), Jimmy Dorsey (1945) and Benny Goodman (1945–1946). A teenaged Getz came to prominence in Woody Herman's Second Herd (1947–1949), where he was featured alongside fellow saxophonists Zoot Sims, Herbie Steward and Serge Chaloff as the vaunted Four Brothers.

Getz toured in Norman Granz's Jazz at the Philharmonic revue before forming his own first quartet in 1950 featuring pianist Al Haig, bassist Tommy Potter and drummer Roy Haynes. In 1951, Getz forged an important musical partnership with the great bop guitarist Jimmy Raney and the following year joined guitar great Johnny Smith on a hit recording of "Moonlight in Vermont." Through the 1950s, he had encounters with trombonists Bob Brookmeyer and J.J. Johnson, pianist Oscar Peterson and baritone saxophonist Gerry Mulligan. During an extended stay in Europe from 1958 to 1960, he also collaborated with Danish and Swedish jazz musicians.

185 | Tenor sax great Stan Getz at the 1991
Banlieues Bleues - Jazz Festival in Paris, France.

186 | Vintage 1950s promo shot of Stan Getz posing with his tenor saxophone, during his run with Norman Granz's Jazz at the Philharmonic concerts.

187 | Tenor sax star Stan Getz jamming with "The King of Swing" Benny Goodman at the Mosque Theater in Newark, New Jersery, on New Year's Eve 1945.

Upon returning to the United States in 1960, Getz recorded the ambitious big band outing *Focus* with compositions and arrangements by Eddie Sauter. But it was 1962's *Jazz Samba* that brought him wider recognition beyond the jazz cognoscenti. And 1963's *Getz/Gilberto* made him an international star. Getz's working quintet during the mid-1960s included guitarist Jim Hall, bassist Steve Swallow and drummer Roy Haynes. Two 1970s landmarks included 1972's *Captain Marvel* (with pianist Chick Corea, bassist Stanley Clarke and drummer Tony Williams) and 1975's *The Peacocks* (with pianist Jimmy Rowles, bassist Buster Williams and drummer Elvin Jones). Getz also investigated fusion music on 1977's *Another World* and 1978's *Children of the World* (which featured him playing through an Echoplex) before returning to a purely acoustic setting through the 1980s.

Getz's final recording, a two-CD set of intimate duets with pianist Kenny Barron entitled *People Time*, was recorded in March 1991, just three months before the saxophonist's death from liver cancer on 6 June 1991.

DAVE BRUBECK

ADVENTURES IN TIME

A legendary, revered figure in jazz, pianist-composer Dave Brubeck injected a new rhythmic sensibility into the music with such ground-breaking recordings as the platinum-selling *Time Out* (which contained such tricky time signature pieces as the 5/4 "Take Five" and the 9/8 piece "Blue Rondo a la Turk"), 1961's *Time Further Out* (including the 7/4 "Unsquare Dance"), 1962's *Time in Outer Space* (dedicated to Apollo astronaut John Glenn) and 1964's *Time Change* (with the 11/4 piece "World's Fair"). Accompanying Brubeck on those essential recordings were drummer Joe Morello, bassist Eugene Wright and his right-hand man, alto saxophonist Paul Desmond (whose signature tone was once described as sounding "like a dry martini"). Enormously popular throughout his long and illustrious career, Brubeck's prolific recorded output has included commissioned operas and orchestral works as well as quartet, octet and solo piano releases.

Brubeck was born on 6 December 1920 in Concord, California. His father was a cattle rancher and his mother, who had dreams of becoming a concert pianist, taught piano to students in her home for extra money. Early on, young Brubeck took lessons with his mother and later studied music at the College of the Pacific from 1938 to 1942. After serving four years in the Army, he returned to California and continued his musical education at Mills College. There he studied with the French composer Darius Milhaud, who sparked Brubeck's interest in fugues, counterpoint and polytonality.

Brubeck helped establish Fantasy Records out of Berkeley, California. His first recording for the label in 1949, an experimental octet outing comprised of fellow students from Mills College, was full of complex time signatures and polytonality. He later formed a working trio, with drummer-vibraphonist Cal Tjader and bassist Ron Crotty, that gained popularity around the San Francisco Bay Area. By 1951, Brubeck had been persuaded by alto saxophonist Paul Desmond to make the trio a quartet and a sound was born. Following a long residency at San Francisco's Black Hawk, they gained widespread popularity by touring college campuses around the country. Successful recordings like 1953's *Jazz at the College of the Pacific* and 1954's Columbia debut, *Jazz Goes to College*, led to Brubeck being featured on the cover of *Time* magazine on 8 November 1954, the second jazz musician to be so honored (the first was Louis Armstrong, who appeared on the cover in 1949). The lineup for the classic Dave Brubeck Quartet was finally cemented when drummer Joe Morello and bassist Eugene Wright joined in 1955.

191 | Pianist-composer Dave Brubeck performing with his trio in New York City's Central Park in 1975.

Brubeck and Desmond remained inseparable musical partners through 1967, when the quartet was disbanded. Desmond and Brubeck were reunited on 1975's intimate *The Duets* and on a few Brubeck Quartet reunion concerts held shortly before the saxophonist died of lung cancer on 30 May 1977.

Through the 1970s, Brubeck composed extended orchestral and choral works while continuing to tour with Two Generations of Brubeck, featuring his sons Darius on keyboards, Dan on drums, and Chris on electric bass. The 1980s and 1990s saw him composing orchestral works and ballet scores while also making concert appearances and recordings with smaller jazz groups. In 2006, at the 49th Monterey Jazz Festival, Brubeck debuted *Cannery Row Suite*, a jazz opera based on John Steinbeck's novel. In 2010, Brubeck was the subject of the Clint Eastwood-produced documentary *In His Own Sweet Way*. At 90 years young, he remains a vigorously swinging player and inventive composer.

192 | Dave Brubeck's first quartet, circa 1953, with alto saxophonist Paul Desmond, drummer Joe Dodge and bassist Bob Bates.

193 | Dave Brubeck performing with his quartet, 1960, with drummer Joe Morello and bassist Eugene Wright (pictured) and alto saxophonist Paul Desmond.

CHET BAKER

POIGNANT TONES, RAVAGED LIFE

One of the most visible exponents of the West Coast cool school of jazz during the 1950s, trumpeter-vocalist Chet Baker played and sang in an intimate style that was far more restrained and mellow than incendiary boppers like Dizzy Gillespie and Fats Navarro or aggressively blowing hard boppers like Clifford Brown and Freddie Hubbard. Part of Baker's appeal was his matinee idol looks, which made him a natural for magazine covers during the 1950s. But his addiction to heroin would rob him of both his chops and his photogenic appeal later in his career. Once a handsome young man with a sweet-toned horn — the great white hope of West Coast jazz — he was strung out, physically ravaged and broke when he died tragically in 1988.

Born Chesney Henry Baker Jr. on 23 December 1929 in Yale, Oklahoma, his father was a guitarist who played in local country and western bands. At age 10, the family moved to Southern California. Trying to encourage his son to pursue music, Chesney Sr. bought Chet a trombone. But the 12-year-old found it difficult to handle, so he eventually switched to trumpet. Dropping out of high school at age 17 to join the Army, Baker was stationed in Berlin and played trumpet in the Army Band. Following his discharge from the Army, he frequented San Francisco jazz clubs like Bop City and The Blackhawk. After a brief apprenticeship with Stan Getz, Baker was chosen by bebop icon Charlie Parker for a series of West Coast gigs, which instantly elevated his profile.

In 1952, Baker joined Gerry Mulligan's piano-less quartet, considered a revolutionary idea in jazz at the time. Their version of the melancholy ballad "My Funny Valentine," featuring a particularly expressive Baker trumpet solo, became a hit and was, forever after, associated with the trumpeter. When Mulligan went to jail in June 1953 on a drug charge, Baker formed his own quartet with pianist Russ Freeman, bassist Carson Smith and drummer Bob Neal, launching his solo career at age 25 with the 1954 Pacific Jazz album *Chet Baker Sings*. Following its release, Baker was named Best New Trumpet Talent in the *Down Beat* Critics Poll.

In 1955, Baker parlayed his good looks into a Hollywood film debut, *Hell's Horizon*. He returned to the jazz scene in 1956 with a hard boppish quartet featuring former Jazz Messenger pianist Bobby Timmons. In 1957, Baker toured with the Birdland All-Stars and later took a group to Europe, eventually settling in Italy in 1959 and acting in another film there. By this time, Baker's heroin habit began interfering with his career. He was arrested in Italy during the summer of 1960 and spent most of the decade

195 | Trumpet star Chet Baker in 1953, shortly after forming his first quartet with pianist Russ Freeman, bassist Carson Smith and drummer Bob Neal, launching his solo career at age 25.

in Europe, enduring frequent arrests and jail time for drug offenses. By the end of the 1960s, his condition had deteriorated so much that he rarely performed in public anymore and only recorded infrequently.

By the early 1970s, Baker had stopped playing altogether. He was coaxed out of retirement in November 1974 by a triumphant reunion concert with his old colleague Gerry Mulligan at Carnegie Hall. In 1978, he moved to Europe and began mounting a comeback in earnest, performing frequently and making recordings into the mid 1980s that, despite his ravaged condition, included poignant renditions of plaintive themes like "My Foolish Heart," "I Fall in Love Too Easily," "She Was Too Good To Me" and, of course, "My Funny Valentine." Baker's tragic end came on 13 May 1988, when he fell out of a second-story hotel window in Amsterdam. Heroin and cocaine were found in his hotel room and an autopsy also revealed these drugs to be in his body at the time of his death. Baker's tough, turbulent life was depicted in Bruce Weber's posthumously-released documentary, *Let's Get Lost*, which was described by the *New York Times* as "seductive and unsettling."

196-197 | Chet Baker lounging in the studio, circa 1952; a pretty face and a talented trumpeter who had a tragic fall from grace, culminating in his death in 1988.

198-199 | Trumpeter Chet Baker in contemplative moment in 1977, prior to his move to Europe, where he began mounting a comeback.

"A lot of the gentle singing style of Chet Baker I noticed more than once showing up in my delivery."

Frank Black

CHARLES MINGUS

FORMIDABLE BASSIST
PROLIFIC COMPOSER

An imposing, irascible figure on the bandstand as well as one of the most prolific composers in jazz — second only to Duke Ellington for the sheer scope and range of his writing (trios, quintets, big bands and full orchestras) — Charles Mingus amassed a body of work from the early 1950s through the late 1970s that ranks him as one of the foremost composers of his day. Mingus' prowess with the pen was so profound, in fact, that it tended to overshadow his formidable bass-playing skills. He was also a civil rights activist and a pioneer of the melding of jazz and poetry in the 1950s. Sometimes feared for his occasional onstage temper, which was at times directed at members of his band and other times at the audience, Mingus was physically large and was, by all accounts, intimidating when expressing his anger or displeasure. Prone to clinical depression, he tended to have brief periods of extreme creative activity followed fairly long periods of greatly decreased output.

A proponent of collective improvisation within the confines of his compositions, Mingus' music drew heavily on black gospel music and blues while also drawing on elements of Third Stream, free jazz and classical music. At a time when musicians like Dave Brubeck, John Lewis, Chet Baker and Gerry Mulligan were treading a new path with a more elegant, refined approach to jazz, Mingus' approach on signature pieces like "Wednesday Night Prayer Meeting," "Haitian Fight Song" and "Eat That Chicken" was unapologetically earthy, funky, raucous and audacious.

Born on an Army base in Nogales, Arizona on 22 April 1922, the son of a mixed-race couple, Mingus grew up in the predominantly black Watts section of Los Angeles. His earliest musical influences came from the church and, at age eight, from hearing Duke Ellington on the radio. Beginning studies on trombone and cello, he took up the double bass in high school and studied with jazz bassist Red Callender as well as with Herman Rheinschagen, a former bass player with the New York Philharmonic Orchestra. His early gigging experiences included a stint with Barney Bigard's ensemble in 1942 and a tour with Louis Armstrong's big band the following year. In 1947, he appeared in the recording studio for the first time as a featured player with Lionel Hampton's big band on his own composition "Mingus Fingers."

Mingus later gained national recognition as a member of Red Norvo's trio with guitarist Tal Farlow from 1950 to 1951. Following a move to New York City in 1952, he worked with everyone from Charlie Parker and Dizzie Gillespie to Art Tatum, Miles Davis and Bud Powell. He formed his own Debut Records

with Max Roach and in 1953 their label documented an historic concert at Massey Hall in Toronto with himself on bass, Roach on drums, Powell on piano, Parker on alto sax and Gillespie on trumpet. Mingus also had a brief stint in the Duke Ellington Orchestra in 1953 (he was one of the only musicians ever to be personally fired by Duke).

By the mid 1950s, Mingus had begun to thrive as a composer on the strength of such acclaimed recordings as 1956's *Pithecanthropus Erectus* and 1957's *The Clown*. During this period he also founded the Jazz Workshop, a group which enabled young composers to have their new works performed in concert and on recordings. But it was 1959 — a remarkably fertile year in which he produced three gems in *Blues & Roots*, *Mingus Ah Um* and *Mingus Dynasty* — that certified his place in jazz history.

A disastrous Town Hall concert in 1962 had Mingus over-reaching with an under-rehearsed band on some exceedingly difficult orchestral music (which was posthumously performed, recorded and released in 1990 as *Epitaph*). Mingus had some triumphs through the 1960s, including *The Black Saint and the Sinner Lady* and *Mingus, Mingus, Mingus, Mingus, Mingus* (both in 1963). In 1971, his provocative autobiography, *Beneath the Underdog*, was published by Knopf. In 1974, he released *Changes One* and *Changes Two* with his working quintet of tenor saxophonist George Adams, trumpeter Jack Walrath, pianist Don Pullen and drummer Dannie Richmond. And in 1977, he scored a success with *Three or Four Shades of Blues*, which featured the guitarists Larry Coryell, John Scofield and Philip Catherine. One of his last recordings was a collaboration with Joni Mitchell on her 1979 Asylum album, *Mingus*. By then, he was stricken with amyotrophic lateral sclerosis, popularly known as Lou Gehrig's disease, and was wheelchair-bound during the sessions.

He died at age 56 in Mexico on 5 January 1979 and his ashes were scattered by his widow Sue Mingus on the Ganges River in India. Mingus' rich musical legacy is being carried on by the Mingus Big Band, which continues to perform his music every Monday night in New York City at The Jazz Standard.

204-205 | The formidable Charles Mingus in a promo photo for his acclaimed 1959 Columbia Records album *Mingus Ah Um*. **206-207 |** Sheet music spread across several music stands for a Charles Mingus quintet performance at the Nimes Ampitheater in France, 15 July 1977.

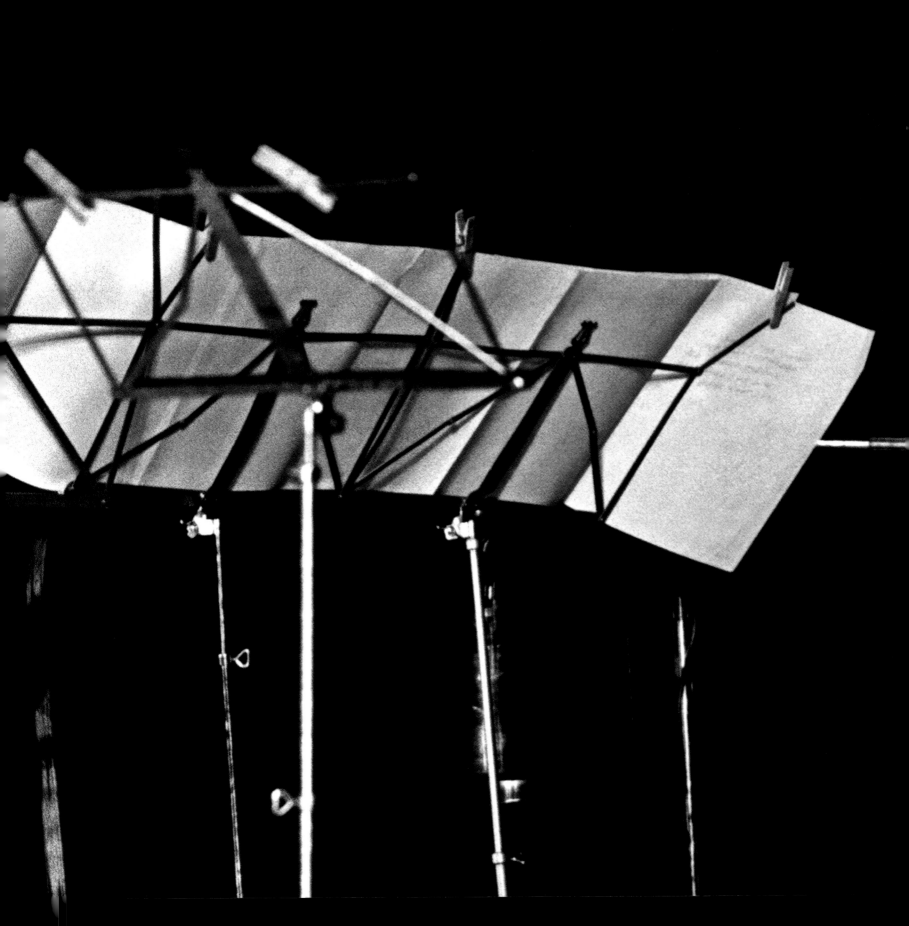

ORNETTE COLEMAN

SAX REVOLUTIONARY
FREE JAZZ ICON

A true musical visionary, alto saxophonist-composer Ornette Coleman revolutionized jazz in the late 1950s, paving the way for the avant-garde movement. An uncannily intuitive, melodic improviser, Coleman's iconoclastic stance has won him legions of fans all over the world and earned him a Grammy Award for Lifetime Achievement. At age 81, his pungent, keening alto sound remains one of the most provocative and compelling voices in jazz.

In his book "Jelly Roll, Jabbo & Fats: 19 Portraits in Jazz," the eminent jazz critic Whitney Balliett perfectly describes Coleman's unique approach: "His melodies are in odd lengths and shapes, and are distinguished for their lyrical beauty and for their sheer graceful irregularity. He has cast aside chords and keys and harmony and conventional tonality. His solos slide from key to key, and he uses non-tempered notes. His time changes continually — from four-four beat to double time to an irregular legato to a floating, disembodied time. Coleman does not improvise on a theme or a set of chords. Instead, he will start from a series of notes, a scale, a rhythmic cluster, an area of pitch, a mood. Coleman's solos are multi-layered and hypnotic. They move melodically with such freedom and originality and surprise that they form an independent music. It is also close to a vocal music, for he tries — with a variety of instrumental cries and mutters and moans and whispers — to approximate the human voice."

Born in Fort Worth, Texas on 9 March 1930, Coleman began performing on tenor sax in R&B bands around Texas and Louisiana. In 1949, he joined Pee Wee Crayton's traveling jump blues band, which brought him to Los Angeles, where he later relocated in 1953. He worked as an elevator operator while trying to make inroads on L.A.'s Central Avenue scene, but his unorthodox approach to the alto sax was roundly dismissed by prominent players on the scene. By 1955, Coleman had begun experimenting with a crew of like-minded young musicians, including trumpeter Don Cherry, bassist Charlie Haden, drummer Billy Higgins and pianist Paul Bley. They jammed freely at the Hillcrest Club, a kind of laboratory scene similar to that which the bebop pioneers had had at Minton's Playhouse in Harlem during the early 1940s. In March, 1958, Coleman recorded his debut, *Something Else!* The watershed year of 1959 saw the release of his *Tomorrow is the Question!* and the prophetically-titled *The Shape of Jazz to Come*, which included Coleman gems like "Focus on Sanity," "Peace" and the hauntingly beautiful "Lonely Woman." By the summer of 1959, Coleman's quartet of Cherry, Haden and Higgins had relocated to New York and by November they had begun a residency at the Five Spot Café, where they quickly created a huge buzz. At

209 | Jazz revolutionary Ornette Coleman at the 2010 North Sea Jazz Festival; still on the cutting edge some 50 years after his prophetically-titled *The Shape of Jazz to Come*.

the time, critic Martin Williams wrote in *Jazz Review*: "What Ornette Coleman is playing will affect the whole character of jazz music profoundly and persuasively." And yet, Coleman's revolutionary music created a great divide in the jazz community, with as many respected musicians and critics railing against it as praising it.

Through the early 1960s, Coleman amassed an impressive body of work on a series of Atlantic recordings, including *The Art of the Improvisers*, *This is Our Music*, *Change of the Century* and the provocative *Free Jazz: A Collective Improvisation* which featured a double quartet including Cherry and Freddie Hubbard on trumpets, Haden and Scott LaFaro on basses, Higgins and Ed Blackwell on drums, Eric Dolphy on bass clarinet and himself on alto sax. He subsequently formed a new trio, featuring bassist David Izenzon and drummer Charles Moffett, which recorded *At the Golden Circle Stockholm* for Blue Note. In 1968, he assembled his second great quartet, featuring bassist Jimmy Garrison, drummer Elvin Jones and tenor saxophonist Dewey Redman, for two potent Blue Note recordings — *New York Is Now* and *Love Call*.

In 1972, Coleman explored his interest in strings on the orchestral piece *Skies of America*. By the mid 1970s, he had traveled to Morocco and jammed with the Master Musicians of Joujouka, who appeared on his 1976 landmark *Dancing in Your Head*. Coleman later embraced the sound of electric guitars and electric basses with his dynamic, funk-inspired harmolodic Prime Time ensemble, which released 1979's *Of Human Feelings*, 1987's *In All Languages* and 1988's *Virgin Beauty* (featuring a guest appearance by Grateful Dead guitarist Jerry Garcia). In 1985, he collaborated with guitarist Pat Metheny on the controversial *Song X*. Since 2005, Coleman's working quartet has consisted of his son Denardo on drums and a two-bass tandem featuring the classically trained Tony Falanga. That unit appears on 2006's *Sound Grammar*, which received a Pulitzer Prize for music.

210-211 | Avant-garde figurehead Ornette Coleman, lounging backstage with his alto saxophone, circa 1987.

212 | Saxophonist Ornette Coleman performing with bassist Tony Falanga at the 40th Montreux Jazz Festival in 2006 in an "Hommage to Neshui Ertegun." **213 |** Close-up shot of Ornette Coleman's signature cream-colored acrylic plastic alto saxophone manufactured by the British Grafton company, at the 2010 North Sea Jazz Festival in Rotterdam.

"I asked my mother could I have an instrument. She said, 'Well if you go out and save your money.' So I went and got - I made me a shine box. I went out and started shining shoes, and I'd bring whatever I made."

Ornette Coleman

JIMMY SMITH

THE ORIGINAL HAMMOND B-3 BURNER

The undisputed heavyweight champion of the Hammond B-3 organ, Jimmy Smith revolutionized the cumbersome 400-pound instrument in the early 1950s by bridging the gap between bebop and blues with his earthy virtuosity. Although he wasn't the first to play the electric organ in a jazz context (Fats Waller, Milt Buckner and Wild Bill Davis had all done that), Smith took the hulking B-3 to places that it had never been before. His burning right-handed flurries on the keys, delivered with confidence and swagger, emulated the alto sax flights of Charlie Parker, while his grooving bass lines and soulful phrasing brought a deep-blue quality and gospel-shout intensity to his music.

Smith could wail in pyrotechnic fashion on bebop staples like Parker's "Confirmation" or "Au Privave," then build to a gospel-tinged crescendo on 'churchy' numbers like Horace Silver's "The Preacher" or his own bluesy "The Sermon." He could create velvety sounds on sumptuous ballads like "Flamingo" and "Lover Man" and get funky on earthy numbers like James Brown's "Papa's Got a Brand New Bag" or his own "Back at the Chicken Shack."

James Oscar Smith was born on 8 December 1925 in Norristown, Pennsylvania, a suburb of Philadelphia. Both of his parents were pianists and his father was his primary teacher. At age nine, Jimmy won first place in a talent competition playing boogie-woogie piano. By age 12, he had teamed up with his father in a song and dance act, performing at various clubs, and on radio shows, in and around the Philadelphia area. Following a stint in the Navy, he attended Philadelphia's Ornstein School of Music, where he studied bass and piano. Smith switched to the organ in 1951 and after a year-long period of intensive woodshedding, he emerged a full-blown organ monster, later debuting at age 30 with 1956's *A New Star, A New Sound: Jimmy Smith at the Organ* on the Blue Note label. Smith's triumphant appearance at the 1957 Newport Jazz Festival helped boost his profile.

A perennial poll-winner, Smith had a string of successful Blue Note recordings through the 1950s and the early 1960s that featured such stellar sidemen as Kenny Burrell, Lee Morgan, Lou Donaldson, Jackie McLean and Stanley Turrentine. After switching to the Verve label, he enjoyed commercial success with 1964's *The Cat*, 1965's *Organ Grinder Swing* and 1966's *Jimmy & Wes: The Dynamic Duo* (his encounter with guitar great Wes Montgomery). He recorded prolifically through the 1970s, 1980s and 1990s for a variety of labels, including second tenures with Blue Note and Verve. His 1983 Elektra album, *Off the Top*, was an all-star session featuring veterans George Benson, Stanley Turrentine, Ron

215 | Jimmy Smith, the undisputed heavyweight champion of the Hammond B-3 organ, wailing with soulful abandon in a 1988 performance.

Carter and Grady Tate while his 1995 Verve offering, *Damn!,* sur-
rounded the organist with a cast of Young Lions on the scene.
Smith had some late career successes in 2001 with *Dot Com Blues*
(Blue Thumb/Verve) and the live *Fourmost Return* (Milestone).
Named a Jazz Master by the National Endowment for the Arts in
2005, he remained actively playing until his death on 8 February
2005. Smith's B-3 legacy has been carried on by such jazz organ
disciples as Richard "Groove" Holmes, Charles Earland, Joey De-
Francesco, Larry Goldings and Tony Monaco.

216 | Organ master Jimmy Smith
getting down to business in concert
with guitarist Quentin Warren, mid
1960s.

217 | Jimmy Smith's right-handed
flurries on the B-3 emulated the alto
sax flights of Charlie Parker while his
grooving basslines and soulful
phrasing brought an inherent
bluesiness to his music.

WES MONTGOMERY
HEIR TO CHARLIE CHRISTIAN'S THRONE

Acknowledged as one of the most important and influential guitarists to have come along in the wake of guitar innovators Charlie Christian and Django Reinhardt, Wes Montgomery brought an unconventional approach to the six-stringed instrument that involved using his right hand thumb for down strokes and up strokes instead of a pick. This unorthodox fingers-on-strings approach allowed Montgomery to get a warm, round sound from the instrument that was instantly recognizable and imbued with soul. His remarkably fluid single note facility and unprecedented technique of using octaves as a melodic device put him far ahead of the guitar pack during the late 1950s. Montgomery's signature octave technique remains one of the most copied guitar styles, frequently employed by such modern players as Joe Pass, George Benson, Pat Martino, John Scofield, Pat Metheny, Larry Coryell, Lee Ritenour, Russell Malone, Mark Whitfield and Kevin Eubanks.

Though he emerged on the scene in the late 1950s as a highly regarded exponent of urgently swinging hard bop (exemplified by such classic recordings as 1960's *The Incredible Jazz Guitar of Wes Montgomery*, 1962's *Full House* and 1965's *Smokin' at the Half Note*), Montgomery ultimately became a practitioner of easy grooving, pleasingly melodic fare that set the tone for smooth jazz. His later recordings like *Bumpin'*, *California Dreaming*, *Goin' Out of My Head* and *Road Song* served as a template for such current smooth jazz guitarists including Ronnie Jordan, Norman Brown, Peter White, Chieli Minucci and Chuck Loeb.

Born on 6 March 1925 in Indianapolis, Indiana, Montgomery picked up the guitar at the relatively late age of 19 and began teaching himself how to play by copying recordings of his guitar idol, Charlie Christian, by ear. He played locally at the Club 440 before touring the Midwest and South with his own group. In 1948, he was hired by Lionel Hampton and remained with his big band through 1950. Returning to his hometown, Wes decided to make music a secondary part of his life in order to support his large family. While settling down to a grueling factory job by day, he continued playing guitar by night at the Missile Club, where he was discovered by alto sax great and talent scout Cannonball Adderley, who brought the guitarist to Riverside Records. Wes' debut for the label, 1959's *A Dynamic New Sound*, was an organ trio outing with fellow Indianapolis native Melvin Rhyne on Hammond B-3 and Paul Parker on drums. But it was 1960's *The Incredible Jazz Guitar of Wes Montgomery*, featuring pianist Tommy Flanagan, bassist Percy Heath and drummer Albert Heath, that established Montgomery as the new king of the six-string and heir to Charlie Christian's throne.

Wes continued to record in small group, straight ahead, settings for the Riverside label through 1963. His stints with Verve (1964–1966) and A&M (1967–1968) — both under the direction of producer Creed Taylor — were commercially successful though dismissed by jazz purists. Wes had just returned home from a national tour when he died, suddenly, of a heart attack on 15 June 1968.

FREDDIE HUBBARD

BADDEST TRUMPET MAN ON THE PLANET

It is said that nobody on the planet played longer, higher and faster than the great Freddie Hubbard. At the peak of his powers, during the 1960s and 1970s, this quintessential hard-bop trumpeter wowed audiences with his peerless chops, bold tones and audacious swagger. His sad decline in the 1990s from a career-threatening lip injury was well documented. As he expressed in the liner notes to his final recording, 2008's *On the Real Side* (recorded at age 70): "It's really something when you lose your chops like that. You feel like a motherless child." Hubbard passed away later that year, leaving behind a voluminous recorded legacy that still stands as the pinnacle for jazz trumpet playing.

Hubbard's technical mastery of his instrument was apparent from an early age. Born on 7 April 1938 in Indianapolis, Indiana, he worked locally as a teenager around 'Naptown' with the brothers Wes, Buddy and Monk Montgomery, later making his recorded debut in 1957 on Wes Montgomery's *Fingerpickin'* on the Pacific Jazz label. In 1958, at age 20, Hubbard moved to New York and immediately began working with such veteran jazz musicians Philly Joe Jones, Sonny Rollins, Slide Hampton, Eric Dolphy, J. J. Johnson, and Quincy Jones. He made his own debut as a leader in June 1960 (*Open Sesame* on the Blue Note label) and in December of that year appeared on Ornette Coleman's groundbreaking double quartet album, *Free Jazz*.

During his important apprenticeship with Art Blakey's Jazz Messengers, from 1961 to 1964, Hubbard played alongside tenor saxophonist Wayne Shorter and trombonist Curtis Fuller on the frontline, appearing on such classic recordings as 1961's *Mosaic* , 1963's *Ugetsu* and 1964's *Free For All*. Concurrent with his tenure in the Jazz Messengers, he also had a string of sterling hard bop releases as a leader for Blue Note, including 1961's *Ready for Freddie*, 1962's *Hub-Tones* and 1964's *Breaking Point*. Through Blue Note's golden years, Hubbard also appeared as a sideman on a number of significant recordings for the label by the likes of Wayne Shorter (*Speak No Evil*), Herbie Hancock (*Takin' Off*, *Empyrean Isles*, *Maiden Voyage*), Bobby Hutcherson (*Dialogue*), Andrew Hill (*Compulsion*) and Eric Dolphy (*Out to Lunch*). The in-demand trumpeter also participated in landmark sessions for other labels by John Coltrane (*Africa/Brass*, *Ascension*) and Max Roach (*Drums Unlimited*).

After a decade with Blue Note, Hubbard signed with Creed Taylor's CTI label, debuting in 1970 with his best-selling *Red Clay*. An artistic and commercial triumph, it was a turning point in Hubbard's career, paving the way for successful crossover albums like *Straight Life* and *First Light*. In 1977, Hubbard changed course from crossover jazz to straight ahead after joining the VSOP Quintet alongside Herbie Hancock, Tony

Williams, Ron Carter and Wayne Shorter, all members of the mid-1960s Miles Davis Quintet. They released four live albums documenting their indelible chemistry on classic Miles material. Hubbard subsequently led his own hard bop flavored groups through the 1980s, then suffered a career setback in 1992 when a serious lip injury (his upper lip ruptured and developed an infection) compromised his sterling chops. He made a comeback in 2001 with *New Colors*, backed by the New Jazz Composers Octet, and in 2006 was named a Jazz Master by the National Endowment for the Arts. He was once again paired with the New Jazz Composers Octet on 2008's *On the Real Side*, released six months before Hubbard's death on 29 December from a heart attack. And though his playing was technically diminished on that final outing, it was still imbued with plenty of soul and the sound of surprise.

HERBIE HANCOCK

Like his mentor Miles Davis, Herbie Hancock has continued to reinvent himself over five decades of music-making. And like the title of one of his most famous recordings, "Chameleon," he has been changing his colors to suit a myriad of musical surroundings, shifting from straight ahead acoustic jazz to groundbreaking fusion, evocative soundtrack work, cutting edge techno-funk and interpretations of modern pop standards.

A hugely influential pianist, Hancock is a sensitive accompanist with an amazing sense of rhythmic invention. Widely admired for his adventurous chord voicings, he interacts intuitively with a soloist's ideas while leaving space and creating a sense of drama within a piece. As an improviser, Hancock has a distinctive linear style that at times is reminiscent of bebop pianists like Bud Powell and Wynton Kelly but also occupies its own unique place in jazz history. His massive body of work as a composer includes such timeless jazz gems as "Maiden Voyage," "Cantaloupe Island," "Dolphin Dance," "The Sorcerer," "Speak Like a Child" and "One Finger Snap."

Born on 12 April 1940 in Chicago, Illinois, Hancock took up piano at age seven and by age 11 had played the first movement of a Mozart piano concerto with the Chicago Symphony Orchestra. It wasn't until a friend introduced him to pianists George Shearing and Oscar Peterson that he became interested in jazz. After studying electronics at Grinnell College in Iowa, Hancock was recruited by jazz trumpeter Donald Byrd, who brought the young pianist to New York in 1961 to record the hard bop album *The Chant* for Blue Note. The following year, Hancock appeared alongside tenor saxophonist Wayne Shorter for the first time on Byrd's *Free Form*. In 1962, he also debuted as a leader in his own right on Blue Note with *Takin' Off*, which introduced his funky hard bop composition "Watermelon Man." A cover version of the tune that same year became a smash hit for Cuban percussionist Mongo Santamaria.

Hancock released a string of superb Blue Note recordings through the 1960s, including 1964's *Empyrean Isle*, 1965's *Maiden Voyage* and 1968's *Speak Like a Child*. He joined Miles Davis' quintet in May 1963 and remained with the group (alongside tenor saxophonist Wayne Shorter, bassist Ron Carter and drummer Tony Williams) for five years, appearing on several classic recordings, including *Seven Steps to Heaven*, *Four & More*, *My Funny Valentine*, *E.S.P.*, *Nefertiti*, *Sorcerer*, *Miles de Kilimanjaro* and *Miles in the Sky*. Although he had flirted with Fender Rhodes electric piano during his tenure with Davis, Hancock dove headlong into the new synthesizer technology as a solo artist, first on 1969's jazz-funk opus *Fat Albert Rotunda* and in an a more fully-realized sense on a trio of experimental sextet outings — 1970's *Mwandishi*, 1971's *Crossings* and 1972's *Sextant*. By 1973, Hancock had paved a new path in funk-fusion with the groundbreaking *Head Hunters*, which sold in unprecedented numbers on the strength of the instrumental hit, "Chameleon." Hancock followed up with the rhythmically innovative *Thrust* in 1974 and the funky *Man-Child* and the live *Flood* in 1975 (all featuring his Headhunters band of saxophonist Benny Maupin, electric bassist Paul Jackson, drummer Mike Clark and percussionist Bill Summers).

224 | Herbie Hancock getting funky on a portable keyboard synthesizer at the Civic Auditorium in San Francisco, 14 April 1981.

225 | Herbie Hancock on the beach in California during the peak of his popularity with his 1970s crossover band, the Head Hunters.

In the 1980s, the ever-evolving Hancock incorporated rappers, turntable scratching, sampling technology and world music elements into cutting edge projects with bassist-producer Bill Laswell (1983's *Future Shock*, which included the MTV hit single, "Rock It," 1984's *Sound System* and 1988's *Perfect Machine*). His all-star 1996 outing, *The New Standard* (with saxophonist Michael Brecker, guitarist John Scofield, bassist Dave Holland and drummer Jack DeJohnette) took a jazzy point of view on a set of tunes by the likes of Peter Gabriel, Stevie Wonder, Sade, Paul Simon, Prince, the Beatles and Kurt Cobain. Hancock's Grammy Award-winning 1998 album *Gershwin's World*, released to coincide with the 100th anniversary of George Gershwin's birth, featured performances by Joni Mitchell, Chick Corea, Wayne Shorter, Stanley Clarke and opera star Kathleen Battle. His experiments with fusing electronic music and jazz continued with 2001's *Future 2 Future*.

An intriguing set of Joni Mitchell tunes, *River: The Joni Letters*, earned him a Grammy Award for Best Album of the Year in 2008. Hancock's most recent release was 2010's *The Imagine Project*, an ambitious collaboration with pop stars Dave Matthews, John Legend, Seal and P!nk, guitar hero Jeff Beck, r&b diva Chaka Khan and his former Miles Davis quintet bandmate Wayne Shorter.

WAYNE SHORTER

THE ENIGMATIC MR. GONE

One of the living legends of jazz, this enigmatic saxophonist has amassed a body of work as a composer that ranks among the most inventive and compelling in modern jazz history. His prolific output during the 1960s, both as a leader and as a sideman with Art Blakey & the Jazz Messengers and the Miles Davis quintet, is staggering. His most famous tunes from that period — "Lester Left Town," "Hammer Head," "Free For All," "Fall," "Nefertiti" and the often-covered "Footprints" — have become part of the jazz canon. His adventurous work in the 1970s with the groundbreaking band Weather Report placed him at the forefront of the fusion movement while his post-Weather Report output as a leader (from a trio of provocative releases in the 1980s — *Atlantis*, *Phantom Navigator*, *Joy Ryder* — to 1995's acclaimed, orchestral *High Life*) furthered his reputation as one of the most forward-thinking composers of the 20th century.

Since 2001, Shorter has been fine-tuning the telepathic chemistry he shares on the bandstand with his dynamic quartet of pianist Danilo Perez, bassist John Patitucci and drummer Brian Blade (captured on 2002's *Footprints Live!* and further demonstrated on 2003's Grammy Award-winning *Alegria* and 2005's Grammy-winning *Beyond the Sound Barrier*).

Born in Newark, New Jersey on 25 August 1933, Shorter learned bebop as a teenager in cutting contests with fellow saxophonists Sonny Stitt and Sonny Rollins. After serving in the Army from 1956 to 1958, he gigged briefly with Horace Silver before joining Maynard Ferguson's big band, where he befriended the group's pianist, an Austrian émigré named Josef Zawinul. Their tenures overlapped for only four weeks but their paths would cross again in the late 1960s on historic sessions for Miles Davis. After leaving Ferguson's band, Shorter joined Art Blakey's Jazz Messengers and remained for five years, establishing himself as a new star saxophonist-composer on the scene.

In the fall of 1964, Shorter joined the Miles Davis Quintet featuring pianist Herbie Hancock, bassist Ron Carter and drummer Tony Williams. They recorded four classic albums together — *E.S.P.*, *Miles Smiles*, *Sorcerer* and *Nefertiti*. Shorter's compositional prowess flourished in Davis' band, and in the looser confines of that freewheeling quintet he developed an impressionistic linear approach to the tenor sax which was steeped in John Coltrane but was more abstruse and made more dramatic use of space. During this incredibly fertile period, Shorter also recorded a string of superb albums as a leader for Blue Note — *Night Dreamer*, *Juju*, *Speak No Evil*, *The Soothsayer*, *Adam's Apple* — while appearing as a sideman on Herbie Hancock's *Maiden Voyage*, Freddie Hubbard's *Ready for Freddie* and Lee Morgan's *The Gigolo*.

227 | Saxophonist-composer Wayne Shorter, formerly of the Jazz Messengers and the second great Miles Davis quintet of the 1960s, blowing his tenor sax at the 2002 Montreux Jazz Festival.

In the late 1960s, Shorter played on the transitional Davis recordings *Filles de Kilimanjaro* and *Miles in the Sky* and *In A Silent Way* — all precursors to the earth-shaking changes to come on 1970's *Bitches Brew*, a landmark album that helped usher in the jazz-rock or 'fusion' movement. Shorter and Zawinul (who had also appeared on *In A Silent* Way and *Bitches Brew*) later formed Weather Report and they released their self-titled debut album in 1971. The two co-leaders presided over several lineup changes during the 1970s and early 1980s, beginning as an esoteric cult band and finally achieving commercial success with 1977's *Heavy Weather* (on the strength of Zawinul's hit song, "Birdland"), 1978's *Mr. Gone* and 1979's Grammy-winning double-live album, *8:30*. During the late 1970s, Shorter forged a special musical relationship with Joni Mitchell by guesting on her *Hejira*, *Don Juan's Reckless Daughter* and *Mingus* albums which showcased his wholly unique voice on soprano sax. He also toured with Freddie Hubbard and fellow Miles alumni Herbie Hancock, Ron Carter and Tony Williams in the acoustic quintet V.S.O.P. Since the disbandment of Weather Report in 1986, Shorter has focused on his solo career, while also appearing on some Herbie Hancock projects (notably 1997's duet recording *1+1*, 1998's Grammy-winning *Gershwin's World*, 2001's *Future 2 Future*, 2007's Grammy-winning *River: The Joni Letters* and 2010's *Imagine Project*).

228-229 | Wayne Shorter with his quintet (from left to right: Danilo Perez on piano, Shorter on tenor, John Patitucci on bass, Brian Blade on drums) performing in London, 2008.

230-231 | A living legend of jazz, the enigmatic saxophonist Wayne Shorter has amassed a body of work as a composer that ranks among the most inventive and compelling in modern jazz history.

JOE ZAWINUL

VISIONARY KEYBOARDIST
FUSION INNOVATOR

In the annals of jazz, Joe Zawinul was a complete anamoly. Raised in the heartland of the European classical music tradition, the Austrian pianist went on to master the art of swing while penning soul-jazz anthems during his lengthy tenure with the Cannonball Adderley Quintet. Later, he trailblazed fusion with Miles Davis and with his 1970s group Weather Report. An uncommonly open-minded musician, he continued to probe new genre-defying musical territory into his 70s.

Born in Vienna on 7 July 1932, Zawinul began on accordian at age six and later studied classical piano at the Vienna Conservatory. Inspired by pianists George Shearing and Erroll Garner, he immersed himself in jazz and by 1952 had become a sideman for Austrian saxophonist Hans Koller. He later played around Europe with his own trio before accepting a scholarship to the Berklee College of Music in Boston, where he relocated in January, 1959. But he dropped out of Berklee after just three weeks to join Maynard Ferguson's big band. His five-month tenure overlapped briefly with that of tenor saxophonist Wayne Shorter, who would pass through on his way to engagements with Art Blakey & the Jazz Messengers and Miles Davis, only to be reunited with Zawinul years later in Weather Report.

Zawinul worked for two years accompanying singer Dinah Washington. In 1961, Cannonball Adderley picked him to fill the piano chair in his quintet. He remained for nine years and contributed several compositions to the Adderley band book, including the hit "Mercy, Mercy, Mercy" and the gospel-tinged "Country Preacher." He also participated in groundbreaking fusion sessions led by Miles Davis, contributing the title track to 1969's *In A Silent Way* and playing electric piano on 1970's *Bitches Brew*.

In late 1970, he formed Weather Report with Wayne Shorter and Czech bassist Miroslav Vitous. Their self-titled debut was a free-floating extension of *Bitches Brew*. Subsequent recordings, like 1974's *Mysterious Traveller* and 1975's *Tail Spinnin'*, became increasingly groove-oriented. 1976's *Black Market* introduced electric bass sensation Jaco Pastorius, whose unprecedented virtuosity and Hendrix-inspired stage presence elevated the band's profile. 1977's *Heavy Weather* became a commercial success on the strength of Zawinul's buoyant "Birdland," his ode to the fabled New York jazz club. After a series of acclaimed albums, and key lineup changes, Weather Report disbanded in 1986.

In 1987, he formed his Zawinul Syndicate, which for the next 20 years straddled the worlds of fusion and world music. He returned to his Vienna roots in 1996 with the symphonic work *Stories of the Danube*. His last album as a leader was the posthumously-released *75*, recorded live on the occasion of his 75th birthday. He died just two months later on 11 September 2007, succumbing to a rare form of skin cancer.

233 | Pianist Joe Zawinul emigrated from Austria to the States in 1959, played with Cannonball Adderley for nine years and recorded with Miles Davis before forming Weather Report in 1971.

CHICK COREA

NO MYSTERY TO HIS MASTERY

A restlessly creative spirit who continues to reinvent himself with each new project, prolific composer and keyboard virtuoso Chick Corea has cut a wide stylistic swath throughout his career, from straight ahead acoustic jazz to cutting edge avant-garde, from children's songs to chamber music to bombastic fusion. As Corea explained, "I decided when I was a young man to make it my primary policy to always keep myself interested and challenged with music." He's managed to do precisely that over the course of five decades, maintaining a standard of excellence that is simply uncanny.

Born Armando Anthony Corea in Chelsea, Massachusetts on 12 June 1941, he began studying piano at age eight and soon came under the spell of jazz pianists like Horace Silver, Art Tatum, Thelonious Monk and Bud Powell. After moving to New York in the late 1950s, he studied briefly at Columbia University and the Juilliard School before embarking on apprenticeships in the early 1960s with Latin bands led by Mongo Santamaria and Willie Bobo. He worked as a sideman with trumpeter Blue Mitchell, flutist Herbie Mann, singer Sarah Vaughan and saxophonist Stan Getz before recording his first album as a leader, 1966's *Tones for Joan's Bones*. Two years later, he recorded the classic *Now He Sings, Now He Sobs* with bassist Miroslav Vitous and drummer Roy Haynes. By the fall of 1968, Corea had joined Miles Davis' band and contributed to such landmarks as *Filles de Kilimanjaro*, *In a Silent Way* and *Bitches Brew*, all of which had him experimenting with electric piano.

After leaving Davis' band in early 1970, following a historic concert at the Isle of Wight Festival before a crowd of 600,000 people, he formed the free jazz group Circle with bassist Dave Holland, drummer Barry Altschul and multi-reed player Anthony Braxton. They toured and recorded briefly before Corea formed Return To Forever in the fall of 1971. It began as a breezy, Brazilian-flavored ensemble (documented on the popular 1972 recording *Light As A Feather*) before morphing into a high-powered jazz-rock quartet with Stanley Clarke on electric bass guitar, Lenny White on drums and Bill Connors on guitar. Their 1973 outing, *Hymn of the Seventh Galaxy*, invigorated the fusion movement. After Al Di Meola replaced Connors in the lineup in 1974, RTF recorded a string of acclaimed albums — 1974's *Where Have I Known You Before*, 1975's Grammy-winning *No Mystery* and 1976's *Romantic Warrior* — that raised the bar on virtuosity in the fusion genre. Corea reconfigured RTF as a large ensemble with four-piece horn section for 1977's *Musicmagic*. He closed out the 1970s with a string of personal projects, including *The Mad Hatter*, *Secret Agent* and the swinging quartet recording *Friends*, while also embarking on a tour of duet concerts with fellow pianist Herbie Hancock that produced two superb live recordings.

Corea's prolific output through the 1980s and 1990s included collaborations with vibist Gary Burton, tenor saxophonists Joe Henderson and Michael Brecker, vocalist Chaka Khan, flutist Steve Kujala and classical pianist Freidrich Gulda. He also toured and recorded with his Elektric Band, Akoustic Band and Origin

sextet before closing out the century with two impressive classical projects — 1996's *The Mozart Sessions* with vocalist Bobby McFerrin and the St. Paul Chamber Orchestra and 1999's *Corea Concerto* with the London Philharmonic Orchestra.

In the past decade, Corea has amassed a string of Grammy Awards, beginning with 2006's *The Ultimate Adventure* (based on the writings of Scientology founder L. Ron Hubbard) and continuing with 2007's *The Enchantment* (his daring duo encounter with banjo virtuoso Béla Fleck), 2008's *The New Crystal Silence* (with Gary Burton) and 2009's *Five Peace Band Live* (co-led by guitarist John McLaughlin and featuring saxophonist Kenny Garrett, bassist Christian McBride and drummer Vinnie Colaiuta). He had a triumphant Return To Forever reunion tour with Clark, White and Di Meola in 2008, toured as an acoustic piano trio with Clarke and White in 2009 and a had reunion of his *Now He Sings, Now He Sobs* trio in 2010. Last year also saw the founding of his Freedom Band (with Haynes, McBride and Garrett) and a new trio with McBride and drummer Brian Blade. Corea continued his flurry of activity into 2011, his seventieth year, by collaborating with Wynton Marsalis and the Jazz at Lincoln Center Orchestra and touring with a new edition of Return To Forever featuring violinist Jean-Luc Ponty and guitarist Frank Gambale.

236 | Corea at a photo session for *Tap Step*, his 1980 album with Stanley Clarke, Bunny Brunel, Hubert Laws, Tom Brechtlein, Joe Farrell and Joe Henderson.

237 | Corea posing for the cover of his 1978 album, *The Mad Hatter*, which featured bassist Eddie Gomez, drummer Steve Gadd, saxophonist Joe Farrell and fellow keyboardist Herbie Hancock.

JOHN MCLAUGHLIN

A BONA FIDE GUITAR AVATAR

A key figure in the development of fusion music, John McLaughlin's pyrotechnic, proto-punk guitar lines fueled seminal sessions by Tony Williams Lifetime, Miles Davis and his own Mahavishnu Orchestra. In a *Down Beat* interview, Chick Corea remarked, "What John did with the electric guitar set the world on its ear. No one ever heard an electric guitar played like that before, and it certainly inspired me. John's band, more than my experience with Miles, led me to want to turn the volume up and write music that was more dramatic and made your hair stand on end."

A bona fide guitar avatar, McLaughlin has, for four decades, maintained a level of excellence on the instrument that is unparalleled. No less than fellow guitar hero Jeff Beck has called him "the best guitarist alive."

Born on 4 January 1942 in South Yorkshire, England, he took up the guitar at age 11, inspired by Django Reinhardt and flamenco music. By the early 1960s, he had moved to London and had begun working with Alexis Korner, Georgie Fame and the Graham Bond Quartet (featuring drummer Ginger Baker and bassist Jack Bruce, who would go on to form the rock band Cream). McLaughlin was also a first-call session musician in London, appearing on recordings by such British pop stars as Petula Clark, Engelbert Humperdinck and the Rolling Stones. In January, 1969, he showcased his technical virtuosity and inventiveness on his brilliant solo debut, *Extrapolation*. Later that year, he moved to New York to join Tony Williams Lifetime, the first band led by the great drummer after his departure from the Miles Davis Quintet. In this raw, jazz-rock setting, McLaughlin became the link between Jimi Hendrix's celestial fretboard flights and John Coltrane's heightened excursions, which he demonstrated on Lifetime's explosive 1969 debut, *Emergency!*, and their 1970 followup, *Turn It Over*. Miles Davis also took note of McLaughlin's singular abilities and recruited him for his landmark *In A Silent Way* and *Bitches Brew* sessions of 1969.

His peaceful, 1970 acoustic guitar album, *My Goal's Beyond*, was like a moment of calm before the storm of the Mahavishnu Orchestra, the tumultuous band he formed in 1971 with keyboardist Jan Hammer, violinist Jerry Goodman, bassist Rick Laird and drummer Billy Cobham. After three scintillating albums with the original lineup — 1971's *The Inner Mounting Flame*, 1972's *Birds of Fire* and 1973's live *Between Nothingness and Eternity* — McLaughlin assembled a new edition of the band and recorded 1974's *Apocalypse* (with the London Symphony Orchestra) and 1975's *Visions of the Emerald*

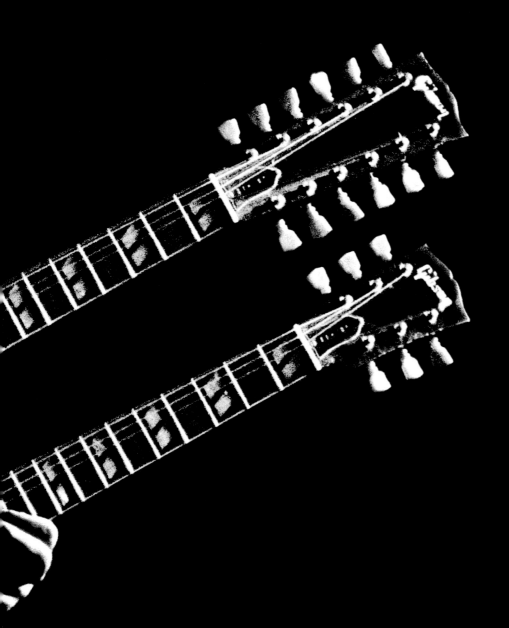

Beyond. Taking a break from the electronic bombast, he formed the acoustic East-meets-West ensemble Shakti, releasing a string of recordings characterized by breathtaking, rapid-fire exchanges between McLaughlin and the four master musicians from India. He exhibited similarly telepathic rapport with fellow guitar virtuosos Paco de Lucia and Al Di Meola on 1980's *Friday Night in San Francisco* and 1983's *Passion, Grace & Fire*.

By the mid 1990s, McLaughlin had returned to his jazzy roots on a series of swinging projects with Hammond B-3 organist Joey DeFrancesco and by 1997 he was back on the fusion trail with his dynamic The Heart of Things band. The ever-evolving guitarist hasn't lost any of his fabled fretboard fire in recent years, as demonstrated by his pyrotechnic playing on 2006's *Industrial Zen*, 2008's *Floating Point*, 2009's *Five Peace Band Live* and 2010's *To The One*.

JACO PASTORIUS

'THE WORLD'S GREATEST BASS PLAYER'

His meteoric rise to fame in the 1970s with fusion group Weather Report was followed by a fall from grace of epic proportions. But during his heyday, there was no one in jazz like Jaco Pastorius. In his prime, the self-proclaimed "World's Greatest Bass Player" had the electrifying soloistic dexterity of a Charlie Parker while his revolutionary approach to the instrument — playing melodies, chords, harmonics and percussive effects — was totally unprecedented. As one admirer put it, "There was bass before Jaco and there was bass after Jaco."

A Pied Piper of his time, Jaco opened the door for a generation of bass players, challenging them to push beyond their limits and discover new possibilities on their instrument. In concert with Weather Report, he provided the links between eras and genres by referencing Bird's blazing bebop ("Donna Lee"), Duke Ellington's classic jazz elegance ("Sophisticated Lady") and John Coltrane's harmonic complexity ("Giant Steps") while blending in Hendrix's cathartic feedback ("Third Stone from the Sun"), James Brown's funk grooves ("The Chicken"), Bob Marley's reggae ("I Shot the Sheriff"), the Beatles' harmonically sophisticated pop ("Blackbird") and Bach's contrapuntal genius ("Chromatic Fantasy"). No one before Jaco had woven together so many idioms into such a seamless package. And he presented it all with rock star charisma and a defiant punk edge.

Born on 1 December 1951 in Norristown, Pennsylvania (hometown of organ great Jimmy Smith), Pastorius grew up in Fort Lauderdale, Florida. Originally a drummer, he switched to electric bass as a teenager and began making rapid progress playing on the South Florida nightclub circuit with such bands as Las Olas Brass, Woodchuck and Tommy Strand & The Upper Hand. He got his first road experience in 1972 with the 12-piece R&B band, Wayne Cochran and the C.C. Riders. By 1976, he had joined Weather Report and rode to international fame with the premier fusion group of the day. That same year, he played on Pat Metheny's *Bright Size Life* and Joni Mitchell's *Hejira* while also releasing his own self-titled debut, a landmark in bass playing. Jaco went on to record six albums with Weather Report, including 1979's live, Grammy-winning *8:30*, before forming his 21-piece Word of Mouth big band in 1982. His albums *Word of Mouth* and the live *Invitation* (recorded on tour in Japan) showcased his compositional prowess along with his peerless bass playing skills.

Diagnosed with bipolar disorder in 1985, his condition deteriorated until the self-proclaimed "World's Greatest Bass Player" was left homeless and reduced to panhandling on the streets of New York City. He died on 21 September 1987 — just two months short of his 36th birthday — from a physical beating sustained while trying to break into an after-hours club in Wilton Manors, Florida.

246 | Pastorius, who revolutionized the role of the electric bass guitar with his soloist approach to the instrument, pictured in 1985. **247** | A bass virtuoso who also brought showmanship to the bandstand, Jaco won over hordes of fans during the 1970s with the premier fusion group of the era, Weather Report.

PAT METHENY
NEW HORIZONS FOR JAZZ GUITAR

In the heat of the turbulent fusion movement of the early to mid 1970s, guitarist Pat Metheny came along to cool things down with a lyrical, warm-toned legato approach to the instrument that one critic described as "the sound of wind rustling through the trees." It was a decidedly less edgy, less pyrotechnic but no less technically proficient guitar style than John McLaughlin had presented in Tony Williams Lifetime or the Mahavishnu Orchestra or that Al Di Meola had offered in Return To Forever. And hordes of aspiring guitarists in conservatories and jazz schools around the world gravitated toward this new guitar star, trying to emulate his appealing style by copying the effects pedals he used. But Metheny's magic was not in any pedal, it was in the hands, heart and mind of this very extraordinary musician; one of the most potent forces in jazz over the past 30 years.

Born on 12 August 1954 in the small Midwestern town of Lee's Summit, Missouri, Metheny grew up emulating jazz guitar greats Jim Hall and Wes Montgomery while also greatly admiring the free jazz of Ornette Coleman. By age 16, he had established his reputation on the Kansas City jazz scene and by age 18 was teaching guitar at the University of Miami. He moved to Boston in 1974 to join Gary Burton's groundbreaking quintet, appearing on the vibraphonist's excellent recordings from that period — *Ring*, *Dreams So Real* and *Passengers*. While teaching at the Berklee College of Music, Metheny began playing around Boston with drummer Bob Moses and electric bass phenomenon Jaco Pastorius. In December 1975, the three traveled to Germany to record Metheny's ECM debut, *Bright Size Life*. His inventive compositions like "Sirabhorn," "Unquity Road," "Midwestern Nights Dream" and the brilliant title track resonated with startling originality while their covers of Ornette Coleman's "Round Trip" and "Broadway Blues" had a personal and very distinctive edge.

The guitarist subsequently formed a working quartet with keyboardist Lyle Mays, electric bassist Mark Egan and drummer Danny Gottlieb. Together they toured around the country in a van, spreading their fresh new sound, which was documented on 1978's *The Pat Metheny Group* and 1980's *American Garage*. Metheny's early off-shoot projects included *80/81* (with Michael Brecker, Dewey Redman, Charlie Haden and Jack DeJohette), 1982's *Off Ramp* (which introduced his use of guitar synthesizer) and 1986's *Song X* (a provocative collaboration with Ornette Coleman). To balance those edgy experiments, Metheny appeased his large fan base with a string of soothing, Brazilian flavored recordings — 1983's *Travels*, 1984's *First Circle*, 1987's *Still Life (Talking)* and 1989's *Letter from Home*. He dug deeper on

1992's *Secret Story*, an ambitious, exotic sound-scape featuring members of the London Symphony Orchestra and special guests Charlie Haden, Toots Thielemans and Akiko Yano. Through the 1990s, Metheny continued to engage in creative collaborations —1994's *I Can See Your House From Here* (with John Scofield) and 1996's *The Sign of 4* (with British avant garde guitarist Derek Bailey) — while turning out more accessible, crowd-pleasing fare like 1993's *The Road to You*, 1995's *We Live Here* and 1997's *Imaginary Day*.

Metheny returned to a swinging jazz guitar trio format on 2000's *Trio 99>00* and *Trio Live* and 2008's *Day Trip*. His solo acoustic guitar offering, 2003's *One Quiet Night*, was a calming breath between two dynamic Metheny Group recordings — 2002's *Speaking of Now* and 2005's *The Way Up*. He also performed luminous duets with pianist Brad Mehldau on 2006's *Metheny Mehldau*.

For 2010's *Orchestrion*, the 17-time Grammy Award-winning artist applied state-of-the-art technology to an age-old music-making process. Drawing on the pneumatically-driven mechanical orchestras that flourished in the 19th century, he constructed a massive robotic arsenal of instruments that could be triggered from his guitar via solenoids. He subsequently toured with eight and a half tons of gear, performing in concert halls all over the world with his sprawling robotic orchestra. Given his risk-taking nature, it is anyone's guess where Metheny's grand vision will take him next.

250-251 | In 2010, the visionary, risking taking artist unveiled his Orchestrion project, which had him triggering a massive robot arsenal of instruments from his guitar via solenoids.

252-253 | Metheny's lyrical, warm-toned legato approach to his instrument was once described by a jazz critic as "the sound of wind rustling through the trees."

"The beauty of jazz
is that it's malleable.
People are address-
ing it to suit their
own personalities."

Pat Metheny

KEITH JARRETT

THE ART OF THE IMPROVISER

One of the most revered player-composers of the past 40 years, Keith Jarrett has produced a body of work that profoundly influenced generations of musicians on all instruments. He is among just a handful of jazz pianists who can consistently fill major concert halls all over the world and his inspired, heart-wrenching performances leave fans swooning.

During his enigmatic career, Jarrett has cultivated the knack of 'disappearing into the music' and his fans go on that journey with him at each concert. Influenced by pianists Bill Evans and Paul Bley, as well as by Ornette Coleman's melodic free jazz and 20th century classical composers Béla Bartók, Alban Berg and Maurice Ravel, Jarrett created a fresh vocabulary on his instrument marked by long streams of singing legato lines and rhapsodic, sweeping moods along with a funky, vamp-based comping style. And while he remains respected by musicians and beloved by fans, his 'enfant terrible' confrontations with audiences about the distractions of coughing and flash photography are well documented.

Born of Hungarian and Scottish descent on 8 May 1945, in Allentown, Pennsylvania, Jarrett gave his first classical piano recital at age seven. By his teens, he had begun playing jazz, inspired by Dave Brubeck. At age 18, he went to Boston's Berklee College of Music, where he studied for a year while playing trio gigs on the local scene. Moving to New York in 1965, he spent four months with Art Blakey's Jazz Messengers before gaining worldwide exposure, from 1966 to 1969, with the popular Charles Lloyd Quartet. The phenomenal success of Lloyd's 1966 album *Forest Flower* crossed over to the hippie audience, gaining the group high profile appearances at The Fillmore and the Monterery Jazz Festival. It was in Lloyd's quartet that Jarrett met drummer Jack DeJohnette, who would become a key collaborator in later years. After leaving Lloyd's quartet, Jarrett joined Miles Davis' volatile group, playing organ and electric piano on such landmark recordings as *Live-Evil*, *Live at the Fillmore East* and *Get Up With It*. (He can also be heard on the Miles Davis compilations *Directions*, *The Complete Jack Johnson Sessions* and *The Cellar Door Sessions*). While Jarrett's contribution on those bombastic records was outstanding, he permanently swore off electric keyboards upon leaving Miles' group in 1971, choosing instead to head down the purist's path. In 1971, he recorded the stirring solo album, *Facing You*, and on 24 January 1975 he performed a daring, purely improvisational solo piano concert at the Cologne Opera House in Germany. It was subsequently released on ECM as *The Koln Concert*, attaining cult-like status through the 1970s and eventually becoming the best-selling solo album of all time (3.5 million copies).

255 | Pianist Keith Jarrett pictured with bassist Cecil McBee during a 1966 TV studio appearance in Copenhagen with the Charles Lloyd Quintet.

In the 1970s, Jarrett developed a distinctive group sound with his quartet of tenor saxophonist Dewey Redman, bassist Charlie Haden and drummer Paul Motian, drawing from the avant-garde while revealing traces of folk, rock, country and gospel music on 1973's *Fort Yawuh* and 1974's *Treasure Island*. Concurrently, Jarrett maintained a European quartet consisting of Norwegian tenor saxophonist Jan Garbarek, Swedish bassist Palle Danielsson and Norwegian drummer Jon Christensen. They explored a different muse that mined Scandanavian folk themes on 1974's *Belonging*, 1977's *My Song* and 1979's *Personal Mountains*.

For the past 25 years, Jarrett has interpreted gorgeous tunes from the American Songbook with his interactive Standards Trio featuring bassist Gary Peacock and drummer Jack DeJohnette. Together they demonstrated near-telepathic chemistry on a string of acclaimed recordings for ECM, including 1983's *Standards Vol. 1 & 2*, 1985's *Standards Live*, 1989's *Tribute*, 1991's *Bye Bye Blackbird* and 2001's *The Out-of-Towners*, *My Foolish Heart: Live at Montreux* and *Yesterdays*. Jarrett's most recent outing, 2010's *Jasmine*, is an intimate duet with his 1970s collaborator, bassist Charlie Haden.

256-257 | Jarrett striking an animated pose at the piano in a 2008 concert celebrating the 25th Anniversary of his trio with bassist Gary Peacock and drummer Jack DeJohnette.

WYNTON MARSALIS

21ST CENTURY JAZZ AMBASSADOR

Since bursting onto the scene in 1982 as a rising trumpet star, Wynton Marsalis has made more than 30 jazz and classical recordings which have won him nine Grammy Awards. He has created music for ballets and symphony orchestras, string quartets and tap dance ensembles as well as for his jazz quintet and 15-piece Jazz at Lincoln Center Orchestra. His extended works include the epic big band composition *All Rise*, the gospel-infused *In This House On This Morning* and *Abyssinian 200: A Celebration*, written for the anniversary of the Abyssinian Baptist Church's 200th year of service in Harlem. He also became the first jazz artist to receive the prestigious Pulitzer Prize in music for his dramatic oratorio *Blood on the Fields*.

A sterling, swinging trumpeter and prolific composer, Marsalis' most important contribution may have been as a high-profile ambassador for jazz over the past 20 years. As artistic director of Jazz at Lincoln Center in New York, he helped lead the effort to construct the first education-performance-broadcast facility devoted to jazz — the Frederick P. Rose Hall (a.k.a. "The House of Swing"), which opened in October, 2004. In his capacity as music director of the Jazz at Lincoln Center Orchestra, the globe-trotting Marsalis has traveled all over the world promoting jazz, just as his hero Louis Armstrong did two generations before him.

Like Armstrong, Marsalis is a product of New Orleans. Born on 18 October 1961, the second of six sons, he exhibited an early aptitude for music, playing his first concert at age eight and performing with the New Orleans Philharmonic at age 14. By 1979, he had moved to New York to study at Juilliard and by the following year had been recruited by drummer Art Blakey to play in the Jazz Messengers. After assembling his first band (which included his older brother Branford on tenor sax), he began touring extensively as a leader. His 1980s output was highlighted by 1982's *Think of One*, 1984's lush strings project *Hot House Flowers* and 1986's *Black Codes (From the Underground)*.

Marsalis' virtuosity, authority and serious commitment to the music triggered a renewed interest in straight ahead jazz during the 1980s, inspiring a new generation of talented young musicians to follow in his wake. In 1996, he was named by *Time* magazine as one of America's 25 most influential people and the following year won a Pulitzer Prize for *Blood on the Fields*. Marsalis ended the millennium with a flurry of activity, releasing an astounding eight projects in 1999 as art of his "Swinging Into the 21st Century" series, including the 7-CD boxed set, *Live at the Village Vanguard*. He debuted on Blue Note with 2004's *The Magic Hour*, followed by *Unforgivable Blackness: The Rise and Fall of Jack Johnson*, his soundtrack to a Ken Burns documentary. His final recording for the label was 2009's spoken word project, *He and She*. In 2010, he released *Vitoria Suite*, recorded in Spain with the JLCO and flamenco guitarist Paco de Lucia, and *From Bille Holiday to Edith Piaf*, recorded live in Marciac with his quintet and French accordian virtuoso Richard Galliano. In 2011, Marsalis received an NEA Jazz Master award.

"I believe in professionalism, but playing is not like a job. You have to be grateful to have the opportunity to play."

Wynton Marsalis

260 | Virtuoso trumpeter and prolific composer Wynton Marsalis in a rare moment of solitude before a performance at the St. Louis Cathedral in 1989.

262-263 | A multiple Grammy-winner as well as a Pulitzer Prize recipient (for his dramatic 1997 oratorio *Blood on the Fields*), Marsalis is one of the most famous and influential figures in jazz today.

JOE LOVANO

IN THE TRADITION, TO THE FUTURE

A perennially poll-winning tenor saxophonist, Joe Lovano has emerged in the last decade as the face of jazz for the jazz cognoscenti. A passionate player who is deeply immersed in the jazz tradition, embodied by the Sax Trinity of Coleman Hawkins, Lester Young and Charlie Parker, he is equally committed to more avant-garde strains of playing, represented by such revolutionary figures as John Coltrane, Ornette Coleman and Albert Ayler. Uncommonly open-minded, Lovano has straddled this inside-outside aesthetic throughout his career. And those seemingly divergent aspects have been well represented in his 22 Blue Note albums. As he told *Down Beat* after winning the magazine's triple crown in 2010's Critics Poll, where he was voted Jazz Artist and Tenor Saxophonist of the Year as well as leader of the Jazz Group of the Year: "I'm not trying to play a different record every time out. But every time you play with different people, it should be a different experience; the music should be something new. That's been my approach all my life in terms of improvising. I can play the same tune every day with different people and it's always going to be new music."

From stirring duets and trios (with the likes of Hank and Elvin Jones, Ed Blackwell, Gonzalo Rubalcaba and Michel Petrucciani) to quartets, nonets, big band outings and full orchestral collaborations, Lovano has tackled all projects with rare authority and conviction. His eclectic discography includes tributes to Frank Sinatra, Enrico Caruso, John Coltrane and Charlie Parker (the latter with his Us Five quintet featuring pianist James Weidman, drummers Otis Brown III and Francisco Mela and bassist Esperanza Spalding). Lovano is also a member of two longstanding ensembles — the Paul Motian Trio (with guitarist Bill Frisell) and the Sax Summit (with Dave Liebman and Ravi Coltrane, who replaced charter member Michael Brecker). He was an integral part of the all-star SFJAZZ Collective and continues to collaborate frequently with his wife, singer Judi Silvano.

Born Joseph Salvatore Lovano on 29 December 1952 in Cleveland, Ohio, he grew up under the tutelage of his tenor saxophonist father, Tony "Big T" Lovano, who introduced him to the music of such iconic figures as Miles Davis, Charlie Parker, Lester Young, Sonny Rollins, Sonny Stitt, Tadd Dameron and many others. He gained his first road experience in 1974 with organist Dr. Lonnie Smith, then apprenticed in Woody Herman's big band in the mid 1970s before joining the Mel Lewis Orchestra in 1980. He began playing in Paul Motian's trio in 1981, then joined John Scofield's working quartet in 1989, remaining a key member through 1993. Lovano debuted as a leader with 1985's *Tones, Shapes and Colors* on the Italian Soul Note label. He launched his tenure on Blue Note with 1990's *Landmarks*.

At age 58, Lovano continues to bring boundless enthusiasm and a sense of adventure to the bandstand every time he hits. As he told *Down Beat*: "In today's world of music, each situation fuels the next for me. I thrive in that energy. The collaboration of sharing the stage and sharing the musical moment with whatever ensemble is something I've always strived for."

"To live in the World of Music
is a Blessing and Jazz is the most
Beautiful Flower in that world !!!!"

Joe Lovano

INDEX

A

Abdul-Malik, Ahmed, 172
Abrams, Muhal Richard, 14
Abbuehl, Susanne, 15
Adams, George, 205
Adderley, Cannonball, 13, 104, 218, 232, 232c
Akiyoshi, Toshiko, 15
Akoustik Band, 234,
Ali, Rashied, 174,
Allen, Henry "Red", 21
Allen, Steve, 75
Altschul, Barry, 234
Ammons, Gene, 120
Anderson, Cat, 82
Anderson, Ivie, 42
Anna Mae Winburn Orchestra, 80
Ansermet, Ernest, 32
Arlen, Harold, 128
Armstrong, Louis, 8c, 10, 12, 15, 18, 22, 22c, 24, 24c, 26c, 27, 31, 31c, 32, 42, 52, 54 60, 64, 82, 88, 92, 98, 118, 128, 190, 202, 258, 258c
Armstrong, Lucille, 26c
Aronoff, Kenny, 136
Art Farmer-Benny Golson Jazztet, 13
Art Tatum Trio, 118
"Austin High Gang", 88
Ayler, Albert, 14, 264

B

Bailey, Derek, 250
Bailey, Pearl, 54
Baker, (Chesney Henry Jr) Chet, 194, 194c, 197, 197c, 201, 201c, 202
Baker, Ginger, 240
Baker, Josephine, 32
Balliett, Whitney, 10, 100, 208
Barker, Danny, 54
Barnes, George, 80
Barnet, Charlie, 72, 106
Barons of Rhythm, 66
Barron, Kenny, 187
Bartók, Béla, 254
Basie, (William) Count, 12, 16, 62, 66, 66c, 69, 69c, 80, 103, 104, 109, 128, 136
Bates, Bob, 193c
Battle, Kathleen, 225
Bechet, Sidney, 10, 17, 21, 32, 32c, 35, 35c, 36c, 174
Beck, Jeff, 225, 240
Beiderbecke, (Leon Bismark) Bix, 38, 38c, 41c, 98
Beirach, Richie, 158
Bellson, Louie, 70, 120
Bennett, Tony, 31, 161
Benny Goodman Orchestra, 70, 80, 88
Benny Goodman Quartet, 90
Benny Goodman Sextet, 80, 80c
Benson, George, 214, 218
Berg, Alban, 254
Berg, Bob, 180
Berigan, Bunny, 136
Berlin, Irving, 128
Berne, Tim, 15
Bernstein, Artie, 80
Bernstein, Leonard, 136
Bigard, Barney, 202
Billy Eckstine Orchestra, 125c, 144
Black, Frank, 201
Blackwell, Ed, 211, 264
Blade, Brian, 226, 229c, 237
Blakey, Art, 10, 13, 70, 106, 120, 176, 176c, 178, 178c, 180, 220, 226, 232, 254, 258
Blanchard, Terence, 176
Bley, Paul, 208, 254

Blue Devils, 66, 103, 144
Blue Five recording group, 60
Blythe, Arthur, 15
Bobo, Willie, 234
Bolden, Charles "Buddy", 11
Bona, Richard, 15
Bonfa, Luiz, 184
Bostic, Earl, 172
Boswell, Connie, 22
Brahem, Anour, 15
Braxton, Anthony, 14, 140, 234
Brechtlein, Tom, 237c
Brecker, Randy, 176, 180
Brecker, Michael, 180, 225, 234, 248, 264
Brookmeyer, Bob, 184
Brown, Cameron, 176
Brown, Clifford, 13, 120, 138, 138c, 156, 164, 174, 176, 194
Brown, James, 214, 244
Brown, Norman, 218
Brown, Otis III, 264
Brown, Ray, 120, 128, 130c, 164
Brubeck, Chris, 193
Brubeck, Dan, 193
Brubeck, Darius, 193
Brubeck, Dave, 13, 62, 190, 190c, 193, 193c, 202, 254
Bruce, Jack, 240
Brunel, Bunny, 237c
Buckner, Milt, 214
Buddy Rich Big Band, 136
Bunnett, Jane, 15
Burns, Ken, 258
Burrell, Kenny, 174, 214
Burton, Gary, 234, 237, 248
Byas, Don, 66, 98
Byrd, Charlie, 184
Byrd, Donald, 176, 222
Byron, Don, 15

C

Callender, Red, 202
Calloway, (Cabell) Cab, 12, 52, 52c, 54, 54c, 57, 57c, 58c, 100, 106
Cannonball Adderley Quintet, 232
Carlisle, Una Mae, 62
Carmichael, Hoagy, 24
Carter, Benny, 64, 70, 98, 106, 118, 128, 138
Carter, Betty, 82
Carter, Ron, 144, 164, 217, 221, 222, 226, 229
Caruso, Enrico, 264
Catlett, Big Sid, 32, 176
Catherine, Philip, 205
Chaloff, Serge, 184
Chambers, Paul, 144, 172
Chaput, Roger, 64
Charlap, Bill, 158, 180
Charles Lloyd Quartet, 254
Charles Lloyd Quintet, 254c
Cherry, Don, 164, 208, 211
Chestnut, Cyrus, 180
Chicago Symphony Orchestra, 222
Chick Webb Orchestra, 70, 128
Christensen, Jon, 257
Christian, Charlie, 80, 80c, 100, 114, 218
Circle, free jazz group, 234
Clarence Williams Blue Five, 32
Clark, Mike, 222
Clark, Petula, 240
Clarke, Kenny, 12, 80, 103, 114, 138, 156
Clarke, Stanley, 187, 225, 234, 234c, 237, 237c
Clayton, Buck, 66
Cleveland, Jimmy, 82
Clifford Brown-Max Roach Quartet, 13
Cobb, Arnett, 82

Cobham, Billy, 180, 240
Cochran, Wayne, 244
Colaiuta, Vinnie, 237
Cole, Cozy, 70
Cole, Nat "King", 103, 180
Coleman, Denardo, 211
Coleman, Ornette, 10, 13, 14, 164, 208, 208c, 211, 211c, 212c, 213, 220, 248, 254, 264
Coleman, Steve, 15, 104
Coltrane, John, 10, 13, 14, 32, 144, 164, 172, 172c, 174, 174c, 184, 220, 226, 240, 244, 264
Coltrane, Ravi, 264
Condon, Eddie, 35, 38, 88, 90
Connors, Bill, 234
Coogan, Jackie, 136
Cook, Will Marion, 32
Cootie Williams Orchestra, 156
Copland, Marc, 158
Corea, (Armando Anthony) Chick, 14, 118, 136, 144, 158, 162, 180, 187, 225, 234 234c, 237, 237c, 239c, 240
Coryell, Larry, 14, 205, 218
Cotton Club Orchestra, 45c
Count Basie Orchestra, 66, 70, 103, 103c, 120, 128
Crayton, Pee Wee, 208
Cream rock band, 240
Creole Dancing Revue, aka Frank Sebastian's Cotton Club Cuties, 63c
Creole Jazz Band, 12, 18, 22, 88, 103
Critics Poll, 264
Crosby, Bing, 22, 24, 38
Crosby, Israel, 80
Crotty, Ron, 190
CTI label, 220

D

D'Rivera, Paquito, 15
Dameron, Tadd, 264
Danielsson, Palle, 257
Dave Brubeck Quartet, 190, 193
Davis, Art, 140
Davis, Eddie "Lockjaw", 66
Davis, Miles, 10, 13, 14, 103, 138, 138c, 144, 144c, 147, 147c, 152c, 156, 158, 164, 172, 174, 176, 184, 202, 222, 222c, 226, 229, 232, 232c, 234, 240, 254, 264
Davis, Steve, 176
Davis, Wild Bill, 214
Davison, Wild Bill, 90
de Koenigswarter, Baroness Pannonica, 114
de Lucia, Paco, 243, 258
De Oosterpoort, Groningen, 234c
de Paris, Sidney, 21
De Vito, Maria Pia, 15
Debrest, Spanky, 176
DeFrancesco, Joey, 217, 243
DeFranco, Buddy, 118
DeJohnette, Jack, 225, 254, 257, 257c
Desmond, Paul, 13, 190, 193, 193c
Di Meola, Al, 234, 237, 243, 248
Dixieland Blues-Blowers, 82
Dockery, Sam, 176
Dodds, Baby, 18, 88
Dodds, Johnny, 72
Dodge, Joe, 193c
Dolphy, Eric, 14, 104, 138, 211, 220
Donaldson, Lou, 104, 180, 214
Dorge, Pierre, 15
Dorham, Kenny, 82, 120, 138, 176, 178

Dorsey, Jimmy, 12, 72, 184
Dorsey, Tommy, 12, 72, 136
Double Quartet, 140
Douglas, Dave, 15
Duke Ellington Orchestra, 64, 205

E

Earl Hines Orchestra, 104, 106
Earland, Charles, 217
Easy Mo Bee, 147
Eckstine, Billy, 104, 106, 120, 178
Edison, Harry "Sweets", 66, 118
Egan, Mark, 248
Eldridge, Roy, 88, 92, 98, 103, 106, 109, 118, 128,
Ellington, (Edward Kennedy) Duke, 12, 15, 32, 42, 45c, 46c, 49c, 54, 54c, 64, 66, 69c, 106, 120, 128, 138, 144, 152c, 202, 205, 244
Ellis, Herb, 80, 128
Ertegun, Neshui, 212c
Ervin, Booker, 13
Esquire Jazz All-Stars, 118
Eubanks, Kevin, 218
Eubanks, Robin, 176
Evans, Bill, 118, 158, 158c, 161, 161c, 162, 254
Evans, Gil, 144
Evans, Herschel, 66

F

Fagan, Sadie, 92
Falanga, Tony, 211, 212c
Fambrough, Charles, 176
Fame, Georgie, 240
Fanelin, Vyacheslave, 15
Farlow, Tal, 80, 202
Farrell, Joe, 237c
Fatool, Nick, 80
Favors, Malachi Maghostut, 14
Feather, Leonard, 100
Ferguson, Maynard, 226, 232
Fields, Herbie, 158
Figueroa, Sammy, 167c
Fitzgerald, Ella, 22, 70, 75, 106, 120, 125c, 128, 128c, 130, 130c, 132c, 135c, 136
Fitzgerald, F. Scott, 12
Flanagan, Tommy, 218
Fleck, Béla, 237
Foley, 152c
Fordham, John, 13
Foster, Al, 164
Foster, Frank, 66, 69
4th Dimension Band, 240c
Frankie Fairfax Orchestra, 106
Free Spirits band, 14
Freedom Band, 237
Freeman, Bud, 38, 88
Freeman, Russ, 194, 194c
Fresu, Paolo, 15
Frisell, Bill, 15, 264
Fujii, Satoko, 16
Fuller, Curtis, 176, 220

G

Gabarek, Jan, 15
Gabriel, Peter, 225
Gadd, Steve, 136, 237c
Gaillard, Slim, 100
Gales, Larry, 116c
Galliano, Richard, 258
Gambale, Frank, 237
Garbarek, Jan, 257
Garcia, Jerry, 211
Garland, Red, 144, 172, 174
Garner, Erroll, 176, 232
Garrett, Kenny, 104, 152c, 176, 237
Garrison, Jimmy, 174, 174c, 211
Gatto, Robert, 15
Gene Krupa Orchestra, 88

Gershwin, George, 32, 54, 128, 225
Gershwin, Ira, 54, 128
Getz, Stan, 76c, 82, 161, 180, 184, 184c, 187, 187c, 188c, 194, 234
Gilberto, Astrud, 184
Gilberto, Joao, 184
Gillespie, (John Birks) Dizzy, 10, 12, 54, 80, 82, 90, 98, 104, 104c, 106, 106c, 109, 109c, 113c, 114, 120, 128, 136, 138, 140, 142c, 144, 172, 178, 184, 194, 202, 205
Gitler, Ira, 172
Glenn, John, 190
Goldings, Larry, 217
Golson, Benny, 176
Gomez, Eddie, 158c, 161, 237c
Gonsalvez, Paul, 42
Gonzalez, Babs, 164
Goodman, Benny, 12, 38, 72, 72c, 75, 75c, 76c, 77, 79c, 80, 82, 82c, 88, 88c, 92, 184, 187c
Goodman, Jerry, 240
Gordon, Dexter, 156, 178
Gottlieb, Danny, 248
Graham Bond Quartet, 240
Granz, Norman, 69, 90, 90c, 98, 103, 109, 118, 120, 128, 136, 184, 187c
Grappelli, Stephane, 64
Grateful Dead, 211
Gray, Wardell, 106
Green, Benny, 176
Green, Freddie, 66
Grey, Al, 66, 82
Griffin, Johnny, 82, 140c, 156
Grimes, Tiny, 80, 118
Gulda, Freidrich, 234
Gurtu, Trilok, 16

H

Haden, Charlie, 208, 211, 248, 250, 257
Haig, Al, 184
Hall, Adelaide, 118
Hall, Edmund, 80
Hall, Jim, 158, 164, 187, 248
Hammer, Jan, 240
Hammond, John, 80, 88, 92
Hampton, Lionel, 72, 80, 82, 82c, 84c, 87c, 90, 118, 136, 202, 218
Hampton, Slide, 220
Hancock, Herbie, 13, 118, 144, 180, 220, 222, 222c, 225, 225c, 226, 229, 234, 237c
Handy, W.C., 18
Hanna, Sir Roland, 120
Haque, Fareed, 15
Harper, Billy, 176
Harrell, Tom, 180
Harrison, Donald, 176
Hawkins, Coleman, 64, 98, 98c, 100, 100c, 103, 106, 114, 118, 136, 138, 164, 180, 264
Haynes, Roy, 100, 156, 164, 172, 184, 187, 234, 237
Headhunters band, 222, 225c
Heath, Albert, 218
Heath, Jimmy, 104, 172
Heath, Percy, 144c, 218
Hefti, Neal, 69
Henderson, Fletcher, 72, 80, 98, 103, 178
Henderson, Joe, 234, 237c
Hendricks, Jon, 118
Hendrix, Jimi, 14, 240, 244
Hentoff, Nat, 92
Herman, Woody, 12, 72, 184, 264
Herring, Vincent, 104

Hersch, Fred, 158
Hicks, John, 176
Higgins, Billy, 208, 211
Hilaire, Andrew, 21c
Hill, Andrew, 13, 220
Hines, Earl, 10, 118, 120
Hinton, Milt, 54
Ho, Fred, 15
Hodges, Johnny, 70, 172
Holiday, Billie, 22, 24, 92, 92c, 95, 95c, 97, 98, 100, 100c, 103, 118, 120
Holiday, Clarence, 92
Holland, Dave, 225, 234
Holmes, Richard "Groove", 217
Horne, Lena, 62
Hot Five session, 8c, 12, 22
Hot Seven Session, 8c, 12
Hubbard, Freddie, 174, 176,194, 211, 220, 220c, 221, 226,229
Hubbard, L. Ron, 237
Huey, Steve, 13
Hughes, Bill, 69
Humperdinck, Engelbert, 240
Hussain, Zakir, 15
Hutcherson, Bobby, 220
Hylton, Jack, 98

I
Instabile Orchestra, 15
Izenzon, David, 211

J
Jackson, Maggie, 132c
Jackson, Michael, 52
Jackson, Milt, 82
Jackson, Paul, 222
Jacquet, Illinois, 66, 82
James, Harry, 136
Jang, Jon, 15
Jarman, Joseph, 14
Jarrett, Keith, 158, 254, 254c, 257, 257c
Jazz at Lincoln Center Orchestra, 237, 258
Jazz at the Philharmonic, 90, 90c, 98, 103, 109, 125c, 128, 136, 138, 184, 187c
Jazz Hounds, 98
Jazz Messengers, 176, 176c, 178, 180, 182c, 194, 220, 226, 226c, 232, 254, 258
Jean Goldkette Orchestra, 38
Jenkins, Burris, 54c
Jenkins, Leroy, 14
Jeremy Steig & The Satyrs, 14
Jimmy's Chicken Shack, 104
Jobim, Antonio Carlos, 120, 184
Johnson, Bunk, 22, 32
Johnson, Deron, 152c
Johnson, J.J., 138, 172, 184, 220
Johnson, James P., 11, 18, 118
Johnson, Marc, 161
Jones, Elvin, 164, 174, 174c, 187, 211, 264
Jones, Hank, 264
Jones, Jo "Papa", 16, 66, 118, 136
Jones, Philly Joe, 144, 158c, 172, 220
Jones, Quincy, 147, 220
Jones, Thad, 66, 69
Joplin, Scott, 11, 60
Jordan, Clifford, 140
Jordan, Louis, 12, 52, 70, 128, 164
Jordan, Ronnie, 218
Jordan, Taft, 128
Josephson, Barney, 92

K
Kelly, Wynton, 222
Kenton, Stan, 184

Keppard, Freddie, 11, 32
Kern, Jerome, 128
Kessel, Barney, 80
Khan, Chaka, 225, 234
Kimball's East, Emeryville, 180c
King, B.B., 80
King Kolax band, 172
Kirby, John, 120
Kirk, Andy, 103
Klein, Guillermo, 15
Koller, Hans, 232
Konitz, Lee, 13, 138
Korner, Alexis, 240
Krupa, Gene, 26c, 38, 70, 72, 75, 82, 88, 88c, 90, 90c, 136
Kuhn, Steve, 158
Kujala, Steve, 234

L
La Barbera, Joe, 161
Lacy, Frank, 176
Lacy, Steve, 14
Ladnier, Tommy, 32
LaFaro, Scott, 158, 211
Laird, Rick, 240
Lambert, Don, 118
Lang, Eddie, 38, 64
Lanigan, Jimmy, 88
LaRocca, Nick, 38
Las Olas Brass band, 244
Laswell, Bill, 225
Laws, Hubert, 237c
Le, Nguyen, 15
Legend, John, 225
Les Hite band, 63c, 82
Les Paul, 80
Lewis, George, 14
Lewis, Jerry Lee, 52
Lewis, John, 13, 138, 144, 202
Lewis, Meade Lux, 32, 80
Lewis, Ramsey, 180
Liebman, Dave, 264
Lincoln, Abbey, 138, 140
Lindsay, John, 21c
Little, Booker, 138
Loeb, Chuck, 218
Lomax, Alan, 20
London Philharmonic Orchestra, 237
London Symphony Orchestra, 240, 250
Lovano, (Joseph Salvatore) Joe, 8, 8c, 10, 264, 264c, 267
Lovano, Tony "Big T", 264

M
M'Boom ensemble, 140
Mabry, Betty, 147c
Mahanthappa, Rudresh, 15
Mahavishnu Orchestra, 14, 240, 243c, 248
Malone, Russell, 167c, 218
Mangelsdorff, Albert, 15
Mangione, Chuck, 176
Mann, Herbie, 234
Manne, Shelly, 164
Mantilla, Ray, 138
Marable, Fate, 22
Marley, Bob, 244
Mraz, George, 15
Marsala, Joe, 136
Marsalis, Branford, 176
Marsalis, Wynton, 15, 176, 237, 258, 258c, 261, 262c
Martino, Pat, 218
Master Musicians of Joujouka,211
Mathews, Ronnie, 176
Matthews, Dave, 225
Maupin, Benny, 222
Maxim, Jacques, 87c
Mays, Lyle, 248
McBee, Cecil, 254c
McBride, Christian, 237
McCall, Steve, 14

McCann, Les, 180
McFarland, Gary, 161, 184
McFerrin, Bobby, 237
McGhee, Howard, 116c
McKenzie, Red, 88, 98
McLaughlin, John, 14, 144, 237, 240, 240c, 243, 243c, 248
McLean, Jackie, 104, 214
McLeod, Alice, 174
McPartland, Jimmy, 38, 88
McShann, Jay, 104
Medeski, John, 180
Medeski, Martin & Wood, 15
Mehldau, Brad, 158, 250
Mel Lewis Orchestra, 264
Mela, Francisco, 264
Mengelberg, Misha, 15
Mercer, Johnny, 128
Merritt, Jymie, 176
Metheny, Pat, 15, 211, 218, 244, 248, 248c, 250, 250c, 253
Metheny Group, 250
Miles Davis Quintet, 172, 221, 222, 225, 226, 226c, 240
Miles Davis Sextet, 158
Milestone Jazzstars, 164
Miley, James "Bubber", 42
Milhaud, Darius, 190
Mili, Gjon, 69c, 103c
Miller, Glenn, 12, 72
Miller, Mulgrew, 176
Milles, Marcus, 147, 147c
Milton, Roy, 12
Mineo, Sal, 88
Mingus, Charles, 82, 106, 138, 202, 202c, 205, 205c
Mingus, Sue, 205
Mingus Big Band, 205
Minucci, Chieli, 218
Mitchell, Blue, 234
Mitchell, George, 21c
Mitchell, Grover, 69
Mitchell, Joni, 205, 225, 229, 244
Mobley, Hank, 176, 178
Modern Jazz Quartet, 103
Moffett, Charles, 211
Monaco, Tony, 217
Monk, Thelonius (Sphere), 15, 80, 114, 114c, 116c, 118, 138, 138c, 156, 164, 172, 176, 180, 234
Montgomery, Buddy, 220
Montgomery, Monk, 220
Montgomery, Wes, 13, 14, 80, 82, 214, 218, 218c, 220, 248
Moreira, Airto, 16
Morell, Marty, 161
Morello, Joe, 190, 193c
Morgan, Lee, 13, 176, 214, 226
Morgenstern, Dan, 70
Morton, Jelly Roll, 8, 10, 11, 16, 18, 18c, 20, 21, 21c, 106
Moses, Bob, 248
Moten, Bennie, 66, 103
Motian, Paul, 158, 257
Mound City Blue Blowers, 98
Moye, Famoudou Don, 14
Mulligan, Gerry, 13, 90, 98, 103, 138, 144, 184, 194, 197, 202
Murray, David, 15

N
Navarro, Fats, 106, 156, 164, 194
Neal, Bob, 194, 194c
New Jazz Composers Octet, 221
New Jungle Orchestra, 15
New Orleans Feetwarmers, 32
New Orleans Philharmonic, 258
New Orleans Rhythm Kings, 18
New York Philharmonic Orchestra, 202

Nicholas, Albert, 21
Nichols, Red, 88
Noone, Jimmy, 72
Norvo, Red, 82, 202

O
O'Day, Anita, 88
O'Rourke, David, 16
Ogerman, Claus, 161
Olatunji, Michael, 138
Oliver, Joe "King", 11, 12, 18, 22, 32, 66, 88, 98, 103
Olympia Orchestra, 11
Onward Brass Band, 11
Origin sextet, 234
Original Dixieland Jass Band, 11, 38
Ory, Kid, 11, 18, 21c, 22, 32
Osborne, Mary, 80
Osby, Greg, 104

P
Page, Oran "Hot Lips", 66
Page, Walter, 66, 103
Parker, Charlie "Bird", 10, 12, 80, 103, 104, 104c, 106, 120, 136, 138, 138c, 144, 156, 164, 172, 176, 178, 194, 202, 205, 214, 217c, 244, 264
Parker, Leo, 98, 106, 120, 178
Parker, Paul, 218
Parrott, Nicki, 16
Pass, Joe, 120, 128, 218
Pastorius, Jaco, 15, 232, 244, 244c, 248
Patitucci, John, 226, 229c
Patterson, Richard, 152c
Paul Motian Trio, 264
Paul Whiteman Orchestra, 38
Peacock, Gary, 257, 257c
Peart, Neil, 136
Perez, Danilo, 15, 226, 229c
Peterson, Oscar, 82, 103, 109, 118, 120, 128, 184, 222
Petrucciani, Michel, 158, 264
Pettiford, Oscar, 98, 106, 180
Phillips, Flip, 128
P!nk, 225
Piper, Pied, 244, 248
Pollack, Ben, 72
Ponty, Jean-Luc, 237
Porter, Cole, 128,
Potter, Tommy, 156, 184
Powell, Benny, 66
Powell, (Earl Rudolph) Bud, 106, 118, 138c, 156, 156c, 164, 176, 178, 180, 202, 205, 222, 234
Powell, John Earl, 156c
Powell, Richie, 138, 156
Pozo, Chano, 106
Price, Leontyne, 54
Priester, Julian, 138
Prima, Louis, 52, 75
Prime Times ensemble, 211
Prince, 225
Pullen, Don, 205

Q
Quaglieri, Al, 52
Quintet of the Hot Club of France, 64

R
Randle, Eddie, 144
Raney, Jimmy, 184
Rappolo, Leon, 72
Rava, Enrico, 15
Ravel, Maurice, 254
Ray Brown Trio & Quintet, 130c
Razaf, Andy, 60
Red Hot Peppers, 18, 20, 21c
Reddie, Bill, 136
Redman, Dewey, 211, 248, 257

Nicholas, Albert, 21

Reinhardt, Django, 15, 64, 64c, 98, 218, 240
Reinhardt, Joseph, 64
Return To Forever, 14, 234, 237, 239c, 248
Rheinschagen, Herman, 202
Rhyne, Melvin, 218
Rich, Buddy, 70, 90, 103, 118, 136, 136c
Richard, Little, 52
Richardson, Jerome, 82
Richmond, Dannie, 205
Riley, Ben, 116c
Ritenour, Lee, 218
Roach, Max, 12, 98, 106, 109, 136, 138, 138c, 140, 140c, 142c, 143, 156, 164, 205, 220
Roach, Maxine, 140
Rodney, Red, 90
Rollins, (Theodore Walter) Sonny, 13, 98, 138, 138c, 156, 164, 164c, 167, 167c, 172, 178, 220, 226, 264
Rostaing, Hubert, 64
Rouse, Charlie, 116c
Rowles, Jimmy, 187
Rubalcaba, Gonzalo, 15, 264
Rush band, 136
Rushing, Jimmy, 66
Russell, Curly, 156
Russell, George, 158
Russell, Pee Wee, 38, 72

S
Sade, 225
Salvador, Sal, 80
Sampson, Edgar, 72
Sanchez, David, 16
Sanders, Pharoah, 14, 174
Sandoval, Arturo, 15
Santamaria, Mongo, 222, 234
Satie, Erik, 158
Sauter, Eddie, 187
Sax Summit ensemble, 264
Sax Trinity, 264
Scofield, John, 15, 205, 218, 225, 250, 264
Seal, 225
Second Herd band, 184
Shaw, Woody, 176
Shihab, Sahib, 178
Shorter, Wayne, 144, 176, 220, 221, 222, 225, 226, 226c, 229, 229c, 232
Schuller, Gunther, 138
Schweizer, Irene, 15
Scofield, John, 15, 205, 218, 250
Scott, Tony, 158
Sebastian, Frank, 63c, 82
17 Messengers group, 178
SFJAZZ Collective, 264
Shakti ensemble, 243
Sharrock, Sonny, 15
Shaw, Artie, 12, 72, 136
Shearing, George, 222, 232
Shepp, Archie, 14, 174
Silvano, Judi, 264
Silver, Horace, 13, 100, 178, 180, 180c, 182c, 214, 226, 234
Simeon, Omer, 18, 21c
Simon, Paul, 225
Sims, Zoot, 184
Sinatra, Frank, 136, 264
Singleton, Zutty, 21, 88
Sioux City Six, the, 38
Smith, Boscio, 92
Smith, Buster, 104
Smith, Carson, 194, 194c
Smith, Dr. Lonnie, 264
Smith, (James Oscar) Jimmy, 13, 214, 214c, 217, 217c, 244
Smith, Johnny, 184

PHOTO CREDITS

Smith, Mamie, 98
Smith, Steve, 136
Smith, Willie "The Lion", 11, 18, 118
Solal, Martial, 35
Sondheim, Stephen, 120
Southern Syncopated Orchestra, 32
Spalding, Esperanza, 264
St. Cyr, Johnny, 18, 21c
St. Paul Chamber Orchestra, 237
Standards Trio, 257
Stanko, Tomasz, 15
Stark, John, 11
Steinbeck, John, 193
Steward, Herbie, 184
Stewart, Rex, 54c, 64
Stewart, Slam, 118
Stitt, Sonny, 104, 106, 120, 178, 184, 226, 264
Stone, Sly, 14
Strayhorn, Billy, 42
Streisand, Barbra, 24
Sullivan, Joe, 38
Summers, Bill, 222
Surman, John, 15
Svensson, Esbjorn, 15
Swallow, Steve, 18

T
Tate, Buddy, 66
Tate, Grady, 217
Tatum, Art, 62, 104, 118, 118c, 136, 156, 180, 202, 234
Tavares Silva, John, 180
Taylor, Art, 174
Taylor, Billy, 118
Taylor, Cecil, 13, 14, 140, 180
Taylor, Creed, 218, 220
Teagarden, Jack, 184
Teddy Hill Orchestra, 106
Teddy Wilson Orchestra, 92
Terry, Clark, 109, 140, 144
Teschemacher, Frank, 38, 88
Tharpe, Rosetta, 54c
The Alabamians, 54
The Art of Things, 243
The Cab Jivers, 54
The Missourians, 54
The Washingtonians, 42
The Wolverines, 38, 41c
Thielemans, Toots, 250
Thompson, Lucky, 66, 120
Threadgill, Henry, 14
Timmons, Bobby, 176, 180, 194
Tjader, Cal, 82, 190
Tommy Strand & The Upper Hand, 244
Tony Williams Lifetime, 14, 240, 248
Tough, Dave, 136
Trent, Alphonso, 80
Tristano, Lennie, 13
Trovesi, Gianluigi, 15
Trumbauer, Frankie, 38
Tuncboyacian, Arto, 15
Turrentine, Stanley, 214
Tyner, McCoy, 13, 164, 174, 174c

U
Ulmer, James "Blood", 15
United Nations Orchestra, 106, 109, 113c
Uptown String Quartet, 140
Us Five group, 10, 264

V
Van Gelder, Rudy, 140c
Vaughan, Sarah, 106, 120, 120c, 123c, 125c, 126, 234
Ventura, Charlie, 136
Vinson, Eddie "Cleanhead", 172
Vitous, Miroslav, 232, 234

Vola, Louis, 64
von Schlippenbach, Alex, 15
VSOP Quintet, 220

W
Waldron, Mal, 140, 174
Walker, T-Bone, 12, 80
Waller, (Thomas Wright) Fats, 11, 24, 52, 60, 60c, 62, 63, 63c, 64, 66, 118, 156, 214
Walrath, Jack, 205
Walton, Cedar, 176
Ware, David S., 15
Ware, Wilbur, 172
Warren, Quentin, 217c
Washington, Dinah, 82, 232
Washington, Peter, 176
Watkins, Doug, 178
Watkins, Kobie, 167c
Watson, Bobby, 176
Weather Report, 10, 14, 226, 229, 232, 232c, 244, 244c
Webb, Jack, 132c
Webb, (William) Chick, 12, 52, 70, 70c, 72, 75, 128, 136, 176
Weber, Bruce, 197
Webster, Ben, 54, 98, 103, 118
Weckl, Dave, 136
Weidman, James, 264
Wein, George, 103
Weill, Kurt, 24, 128, 128c
Wellman, Ricky, 152c
Wells, Dicky, 64, 66
Wess, Frank, 66, 69
Wesselhoft, Bugge, 16
Weston, Randy, 142c
Wheeler, Kenny, 15
White, Lenny, 234, 234c, 237, 239c
White, Peter, 218
Whitfield, Mark, 218
Wilkins, Ernie, 66
Willem Breuker Kollektief, 15
Williams, Buster, 187
Williams, Clarence, 60
Williams, James, 176
Williams, Joe, 69
Williams, Martin, 211
Williams, Mary Lou, 80, 178
Williams, Tony, 14, 144, 187, 221, 222, 226, 229
Wilson, Shadow, 172
Wilson, Teddy, 62, 72, 82, 88, 103, 180
Wonder, Stevie, 225
Woodchuck band, 244
Woods, Phil, 104
Word of Mouth band, 244
Workman, Reggie, 176
Wright, Eugene, 190, 193c

Y
Yano, Akiko, 250
Yanow, Scott, 12
Young, Irma, 103
Young, Lee, 103
Young, Lester Willis "Pretz", 66, 69c, 80, 90, 92, 92c, 100, 100c, 103, 103c, 104, 136, 164, 180, 184, 264
Young, Snooky, 66, 82
Young Lions, 12, 15, 217

Z
Zawinul, Joe, 10, 14, 144, 226, 229, 232, 232c
Zawinul Syndicate, 232
Zeitlin, Denny, 158
Zigmund, Eliot, 161
Zorn, John, 10, 15

Page 166 New York Daily News Archives/Getty Images
Page 168 Jordi Vidal/Getty Images
Page 169 Paul Bergen/Getty Images
Pages 170-171 Andy Sheppard/Getty Images
Page 173 Michael Ochs Archives/Stringer/Getty Images
Pages 174-175 Echoes/Getty Images
Page 177 David Redfern/Getty Images
Pages 178-179 Francis Wolff/Mosaic Images/Corbis
Page 181 Clayton Call/Getty Images
Page 182 Sony BGM Music Entertainment/Getty Images
Pages 182-183 Herb Snitzer/Getty Images
Page 185 Guy Le Querrec/Magnum Photos/Contratso
Page 186 David Redfern/Getty Images
Page 187 Frank Driggs Collection/Getty Images
Pages 188-189 The New York Times/Redux/Contrasto
Page 191 Richard E. Aaron/Getty Images
Page 192 Hulton Archive/Getty Images
Page 193 David Redfern/Getty Images
Page 195 Bob Willoughby/Getty Images
Pages 196-197 Bob Willoughby/Getty Images
Pages 198-199 Deborah Feingold/Corbis
Page 200 Luciano Viti/Getty Images
Page 202 Leni Sinclair/Getty Images
Pages 204-205 Bettmann/Corbis
Pages 206-207 Guy Le Querrec/Magnum/Contrasto
Page 209 Rob Verhorst/Getty Images
Pages 210-211 Andy Freeberg/Getty Images
Page 212 Martial Trezzini/epa/Corbis
Page 213 Rob Verhorst/Getty Images
Page 215 David Redfern/Getty Images
Page 216 Express Newspapers/Getty Images
Page 217 David Redfern/Getty Images
Page 219 David Redfern/Getty Images
Page 221 Philippe Levy-Stab/Corbis
Page 223 David Redfern/Getty Images
Page 224 Michael Ochs Archives/Stringer/Getty Images
Page 225 Jim McCrary/Getty Images
Page 227 Fabrice Coffrini/epa/Corbis
Pages 228-229 Philip Ryalls/Getty Images
Pages 230-231 Lionel Bonaventure/Getty Images
Page 233 Luciano Viti/Getty Images
Page 235 Paul Bergen/Getty Images
Page 236 Jim McCrary/Getty Images
Page 237 Echoes/Getty Images
Pages 238-239 Andy Sheppard/Getty Images
Page 241 AFP/Getty Images
Pages 242-243 Jeff Albertson/Corbis
Page 245 GAB Archive/Getty Images
Page 246 Ebet Roberts/Getty Images
Page 247 Keith Bernstein/Getty Images
Page 249 RAFA RIVAS/Getty Images
Pages 250-251 AFP/Getty Images
Pages 252-253 Paul Bergen/Getty Images
Page 255 JazzSign/Lebrecht Music & Arts/Corbis
Pages 256-257 Saed Hindash/Star Ledger/Corbis
Page 258 Toby Madden/Contrasto
Page 260 Joe McNally/Getty Images
Pages 262-263 Fabrice Coffrini/epa/Corbis
Page 265 Kevin Winter/Getty Images
Page 266 Andrew Lepley/Getty Images

Cover: Louis Armstrong and His All-Stars play
in the movie *New Orleans*, 1947. © JP Jazz Archive/Getty Images

BILL MILKOWSKI

Bill Milkowski is a New York-based freelance writer who has contributed to several publications since the 1970s, including Down Beat, Jazz Times, Jazziz, Bass Player, Guitar Player, Modern Drummer, Absolute Sound, Jazzthing (Germany), Guitar Club (Italy) and Guitar (Japan). He is also the author of "JACO: The Extraordinary and Tragic Life of Jaco Pastorius," "Swing It! An Annotated History of Jive" and "Rockers, Jazzbos & Visionaries." Born in Milwaukee, Wisconsin, where he began his career in music journalism, he relocated to New York City in 1980. He relocated to New Orleans in 1993, returning to New York in 1997 and settling in the Washington Heights area of Manhattan, where he currently lifes. Milkowski was named Writer of the Year for 2004 by the Jazz Journalists Association. An avid guitar hobbyist, he is also the proud father of a 16-year-old daughter, Sophia Vincenza Milkowski.

JOE LOVANO

Grammy-winning saxophonist and composer Joe Lovano is fearless in finding new modes of artistic expression. With 12 Nominations and a Grammy for his52nd Street Themes, he has won Down Beat Magazine's Critics and Readers Polls many times as Tenor Saxophonist, Musician of the Year, Jazz Album of the Year and Triple Crowns from Downbeat and the Jazz Journalists Association in 2010. Born in Cleveland, Ohio on December 29, 1952 he attended the famed Berklee College of Music in Boston where years later he was awarded an Honorary Doctorate. Since 2001 he has held the Gary Burton Chair in Jazz Performance and is a founding faculty of the new Global Music Institute directed by Danilo Perez.
Since 1991 Lovano has been recording for Blue Note Records withBird Songs marking his 22nd release for the label. Joe has recorded with a long list of jazz greats including Woody Herman, Mel Lewis, Bob Brookmeyer, John Scofield, Paul Motian, Bill Frisell, Gunther Schuller, Elvin Jones, McCoy Tyner, Ed Blackwell, Dave Holland, Hank Jones, Dave Liebman, Michael Brecker, Ravi Coltrane and many others. In addition, a concerto for saxophone and chamber orchestra was written for him by Mark Anthony Turnage called "A Man Descending". Joe Lovano continues to explore new horizons within the world of music as a band leader and composer.

WHITE STAR PUBLISHERS

WS White Star Publishers* is a registered trademark property of Edizioni White Star s.r.l.

© 2011 Edizioni White Star s.r.l.
Via M. Germano, 10
13100 Vercelli, Italy
www.whitestar.it

ISBN 978-88-544-0604-9

1 2 3 4 5 6   15 14 13 12 11

Printed in China

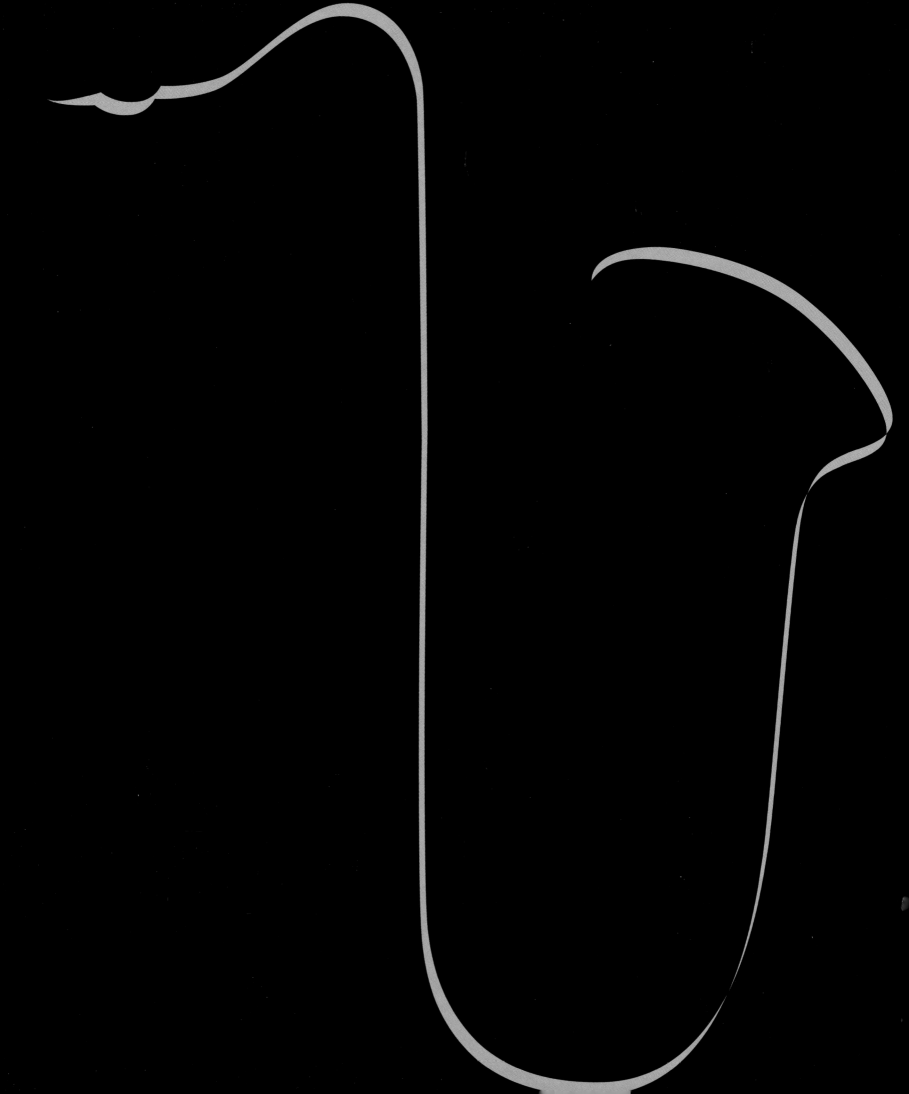